Ruth Weston is a senior dog-training instructor and lecturer in canine behaviour at The Kintala Club, and was the inaugural president of The Australian Association of Gentle Modern Dog Training Instructors. She also runs her own private dog-training business. Together with her late husband, David, she has written three best-selling books – *Dog Training: The Gentle Modern Method*, *Dog Problems: The Gentle Modern Cure* and *Your Ideal Dog: Teach Your Best Friend to be a Perfect Companion*.

Ruth's daughter, **Catriona Ross**, has a Bachelor of Behavioural Science (Honours) and a PhD in psychology. She is a registered psychologist who has worked in various areas of the discipline including counselling, health psychology and, currently, organisational psychology. She is particularly interested in the principles of modern learning theory to motivate and shape the behaviour of both animals and children.

KIDS & DOGS

*Teaching them to live,
play and learn together*

RUTH WESTON &
DR CATRIONA ROSS

A SUE HINES BOOK
ALLEN&UNWIN

*Unless otherwise stated photographs are by Wendy Mitchell,
Dr Tim Adams and the late David Weston.*

First published in 2004

A Sue Hines Book
Allen & Unwin
83 Alexander Street
Crows Nest NSW 2065
Australia
Phone: (61 2) 8425 0100
Fax: (61 2) 9906 2218
Email: info@allenandunwin.com
Web: www.allenandunwin.com

The National Library of Australia
Cataloguing-in-Publication entry:

Weston, Ruth.
  Kids and dogs.

  ISBN 1 74114 394 2.

  1. Children and animals. 2. Dogs – Training. 3. Dogs –
  Social aspects. 4. Child development. I. Ross, Catriona.
  II. Title.

636.70887

Text design by Sandra Nobes
Typesetting by Tou-Can Design
Cover photography and author photograph by Greg Elms
Printed through Phoenix Offset

10 9 8 7 6 5 4 3 2 1

To David Weston
1929 to 1998

Pioneer of dog training using positive reinforcement. Due to
your foresight, commitment and dedication, your dream that all
dogs should be socialised early and trained using your Gentle
Modern Method of Dog Training™ is fast becoming a reality.

To 'Brook'
1987 to 2003

You gave me nearly seventeen years of friendship and love and
taught me so much. You set such a good example to all who
knew you. I miss you so much my golden girl.

Contents

Chapter 1

A dog in the family

Dogs can bring so much to family life. They can be companions in every sense, improving our emotional and social lives in a way that other animals (and sometimes people!) can't. Kids and dogs are natural companions, and this book will show you how to make the most of what can be an extremely rewarding and special friendship. We hope that working through this book will be a very positive experience for you, and that you have many moments when you say to yourself, 'this all seems like common sense!'

Ruth has been fortunate enough to be involved in dog training for over twenty years. During this time many people have asked her for advice about training their child as well as their dog! While Ruth has previously written several books on dog behaviour and training, these books did not provide much information about *human* behaviour. In fact, when we looked at the existing literature on dog training, there didn't seem to be many books at all which covered both dog psychology and child psychology. Given that roughly 50% of families have a dog, this seemed to be a real gap. As a qualified and practising psychologist, Catriona was in a good position to team up with her mother to fill this void.

Although psychology and dog training may appear to be quite different professions, the philosophies of how we interact with dogs and with people in a positive way actually have much in common. Furthermore, the evolution of both dog and child psychology have followed similar paths. The concept of positive reinforcement has been around since the early twentieth century, but it has only been in recent years that so much emphasis has been placed on rewarding the good behaviour of children and on maintaining their self-esteem. You are probably aware

Kids and dogs should be raised in a supportive and loving environment

that in previous generations the physical punishment of children was more acceptable, and the view that 'children should be seen but not heard' was much more common. Similarly, traditional dog-training methods involved correction and punishment, with positive reinforcement virtually unheard of in dog-training circles until we introduced the Gentle Modern Method of Dog Training™ in the early 1970s.

When people are asked about what is most important in life, most answer 'family'. However, when we look at how we spend our time, most of it is taken up with working and sleeping, leaving little time to devote to what we value most. This makes it all the more important that the time we do spend together is quality time. Most families these days want to take on dog training and dog care as a family affair. It is our philosophy that children and dogs should be raised in a supportive and loving environment. By applying effective psychological techniques to motivate and inspire good behaviour, we feel sure that you will experience the very special benefits associated with having children and dogs together in the family.

Why have a dog in the family?

When dog owners talk about what they enjoy most about their pet, most of them mention unconditional love, attention, affection and emotional support. Owning a dog can often provide a unique bond that is uncommon in human relationships – dogs listen, never judge, and accept their owners entirely as they are.

Having a dog as a companion helps people feel safe and secure and can reduce loneliness and anxiety, and walking the dog promotes social contact. Many people find it is easier to meet others when they are out with their dog, as the animal gives people a reason to start a conversation without feeling self-conscious.

As many dog owners will agree, dogs also offer an almost endless source of fun, laughter, humour and relaxation. Dogs are friendly by nature and encourage free and spontaneous expressions of affection and emotion. Most dog owners talk to their pet, with research showing that 94% of owners talk to them as if they were people. This can help dog owners to express their feelings and get things off their chest.

Having a dog in the family means – naturally – that you have to take care of it, and this nurturing engenders a sense of responsibility that helps people feel needed.

A dog in the family can also increase the general physical health of family members. Families with dogs tend to exercise more and enjoy the comfort and calming effect of touching a pet. Studies have shown that companion animals can improve people's physical health, and that dog owners have slightly better health than cat owners.

Dogs are good for our health

The psychological benefits of owning a dog

Dogs can decrease the risk of heart disease in their owners. People with dogs often have lower levels of cholesterol, triglyceride fats and blood pressure than non-pet owners. All of these factors are linked to cardiovascular disease, the number one cause of death in Western countries. In one study, pet owners were found to have cholesterol levels that were 2% lower than average; this equates to a 4% reduction in the risk of heart attack. Another study noted that having a pet in the family is as good a means of reducing blood pressure as reducing alcohol intake or eating a low-salt diet. Having a pet also increases the survival rate of heart-attack victims and may have a protective effect against psychological trauma and grief. For instance, pet owners show less deterioration in health following the death of a loved one compared to non-pet owners.

Families with dogs tend to exercise more

It is not entirely clear why having a dog reduces blood pressure but it is well known that having a calm dog nearby can reduce stress and anxiety. One possible reason for this is that, throughout the evolutionary history of humans, the presence of a calm animal has been associated with safety, and the presence of a fleeing animal with danger. For instance, when humans lived a hunter-gatherer lifestyle, the sudden running of a group deer would have alerted them to the possible presence of a predator, while the presence of calm, grazing deer was a sign that no predator was near. Being in the proximity of fleeing deer would have elicited a stress reaction in humans. This stress or 'fight or flight' reaction is associated with physiological changes including increased heart rate and blood pressure. It is conceivable that the proximity of a calm animal has the opposite effect, reducing physiological arousal.

Why dogs are good for kids

Children who are brought up to have a positive relationship with dogs are likely to remain dog lovers throughout their lives, so kids with a dog in the family should gain a lifetime of all those social, emotional and physical benefits we've just discussed. It has also been noted that pet owners tend to demonstrate more humane, compassionate and positive attitudes to people, animals and the environment compared to those without pets – so the kids aren't the only ones to benefit.

Attachment and unconditional love

Animals accept their owners for who they are without judgement. This can be particularly important for children. The well-known psychologist, Carl Rogers, put forward the idea that children need to receive 'unconditional positive regard' if they are to accept themselves for who they are and develop self-confidence. While it is best that children receive this positive regard from people who are important to them (such as their parents), there is good evidence to suggest that dogs are often considered to be a member of the family and that if parents are unavailable the dog can become a substitute companion. Complete acceptance by a loved dog can help to provide a sense of worth in all children, but particularly in those who have problems at home.

Competence and self-esteem

Having a dog in the family can increase a child's self-esteem and competence. Kids who help care for and train the family dog feel pride and accomplishment, particularly if their parents acknowledge their success. Children often get particular delight out of teaching their dog to perform tricks. Managing such tasks successfully tends to contribute to success in new tasks, helping to establish a positive cycle. Similarly, children who are struggling in other aspects of life (academically or socially, for example) can feel they are achieving something from looking after a dog, and this can reduce the negative impact of their difficulties in other areas. Incidentally, it has been found that children with dogs are less likely to commit crimes later in life.

Independence and autonomy

Learning to become more independent and autonomous is one of the most crucial developmental steps in the transition from infancy to childhood. When children are involved in caring for a dog they can start to see themselves as someone who is depended on, not just someone who depends on others. They're also more likely to go out of their immediate environment, to play and go for walks, without other family members.

A sense of responsibility

As children grow they acquire a sense of responsibility, learning to become self-disciplined and patient. They become increasingly able to understand the constraints of their environment and learn that it is not always possible to do exactly what they want to do at all times. Children

Dogs help to teach kids responsibility

begin to realise they must consider the needs of others and sometimes perform tasks that are not much fun in the short term but yield a longer term gain. Children who share some responsibility for the training and care of a dog not only tend to acquire these skills themselves, but also often try to instil them in their pet! If you're lucky this will help them develop a more realistic view of their own parents and the challenges of trying to parent another. Many parents hear their own words repeated when children encourage the family dog to 'wait patiently until dinnertime to be fed', or tell it to 'practise your lessons before you are allowed to go out for a walk'!

Empathy and the ability to nurture

When caring for a dog, children must learn what the dog needs and then anticipate these needs by interpreting the animal's body language. An ability to imagine how another animal feels, see things from the perspective of another, and communicate using non-verbal means are all important skills that help children relate effectively to others. Caring for an animal also encourages children to be gentle and affectionate. This can be particularly important for some boys who may be less likely to display these sorts of behaviours in our society, and for single children who don't have siblings to care for.

Why dogs are good for kids with special needs

Owning a pet can help children with special needs in various ways. A dog can help a shy child break the ice with other children. When children live in an isolated area with few peers, the companionship of an animal may have to be a substitute for human friendships. Friendship with a beloved

animal can greatly diminish a child's sense of isolation and offer opportunities for play and companionship that adults are not always able to provide.

Pets have also been used in the treatment of specific childhood disorders. Some children with autism have proved more willing to speak to a dog than to a psychologist, and children who had previously communicated very little have been known to share their feelings with a dog. There have even been cases where non-verbal children have spoken as a result of contact with a dog. Adopting a pet as a confidante can help withdrawn and developmentally delayed children learn to express themselves, aiding counselling, treatment and family interactions.

Children and adolescents who suffer from mental illness, including anxiety and depression, may also enjoy many benefits from dog ownership. A dog can increase feelings of security, distract anxious people from their worries and promote exercise. Dogs also make people laugh, which reduces stress and makes us healthier. This can be particularly important for depressed children. Many people find that forming a relationship with a dog is easier than forming a relationship with another person, and this is especially helpful for people who are not very sociable.

Why family life is good for dogs

Many people are surprised when we tell them that some dogs prefer to interact with humans than with other dogs. The bond between a dog and its family is not just a one-way street – dogs too develop an emotional attachment to their family and like having children around. Children usually enjoy playing with their pets and help to keep their dogs active and fit. Many dogs are treated completely as one of the family, and are taken on holidays, thrown birthday parties and given Christmas presents! Dogs can sense when their family members are happy and – by the same token – are affected by tension and stress. A number of studies have demonstrated that dogs can experience physical symptoms such as diarrhoea, gastric upsets and epileptic seizures in response to tension in the home. However this is rare, and a dog that is part of a happy family tends to be a happy, healthy dog.

Dogs love to be part of the family

Chapter 2

Deciding to get a dog

Having a dog in the family has many benefits. Looking after a dog properly, however, is a big responsibility, and choosing to get a dog is an important decision. Many dogs live for at least twelve years – longer for smaller dogs – so this is a long-term commitment. We've devised a series of questions to help you decide whether or not to get a dog. All family members will be affected by the presence of a dog, so make this a family decision. Talking about these issues as a family will help you decide who will take primary responsibility for different aspects of the dog's care. Children will be more committed to looking after the family dog if they have played a role in the decision-making process. Asking children questions such as 'What do we need to do so that we can look after a dog?' will help them understand the dog's needs and the responsibilities of dog ownership. If you decide not to get a dog after working through these questions, your child will better understand the rationale of the decision and be more likely to accept it.

1   Does everyone in the family want a dog? If not, is this likely to be a problem? If you decide to get a dog, would any family member be unhappy? If yes, why? Could this issue be resolved?

2   Do any family members have special needs, for example a dog allergy? If yes, would they be comfortable with a dog in the house? Many children with mild allergies adjust to having a dog around and build up immunity. However, if the allergy is more severe, certain dog breeds such as poodles, labradoodles and smooth-coated breeds such as whippets may be more appropriate.

Certain breeds are good for kids with allergies

Housing

1   Do you have enough space for a dog?

2   Where do you want your dog to live – inside or outside? Dogs that are left outside and not included in family life can become very excitable when people are around. These dogs can also become bored and destructive, resulting in all sorts of problems, from digging and barking to escaping. Be prepared to have the dog in the house the majority of the time when you are home.

3   Where will the dog sleep? Will any family members be jealous if the dog sleeps in someone's bedroom, for instance?

Food

1   What will your dog eat?

2   Who will feed it?

3   Can you afford to meet its food requirements?

4   Will there always be someone home to feed the dog?

Exercise

1   How much exercise is the family prepared to give the dog?
2   Who will exercise it?
3   Will any conflicting demands on your time make it difficult to exercise a dog?
4   Do you have access to places where you can walk your dog? (Preferably off-lead for at least some of the time.)

Grooming

1   How much time are you prepared to spend grooming the dog?
2   Who will groom it?
3   Can you afford to get your dog professionally clipped if clipping is required? If not, who will learn to do this?

Who will groom your dog?

Finances

1 Can you afford to look after a dog? The costs vary
   widely depending on dog breed, quality of food and
   the number of 'extras' you buy. An example of one
   family's bill for keeping their medium-sized dog in
   2004 is shown below. Although this family pays
   more for their dog than is necessary, the table
   gives an idea of the full range of possible costs.

Brook's annual expenses

Item	Annual Cost	Notes
Food	$720	$60 a month for raw meat, bones, tinned dog food, dry dog food, vegetables and treats.
Grooming	$50	For a comb, brush equipment and trimming scissors.
Cost of kennelling	$252	$18 a day during a two-week holiday.
Toys	$50	For various balls, toys and Christmas presents.
Unexpected veterinary bills*	$500	To cover the costs of an infected paw.
Expected veterinary bills	$350	Immunisation, worming, flea control and check-ups.
Doggy day care	$280	$20 a day for two weeks when the family was particularly busy.
License fees	$20	This could be up to $80 if the dog is not spayed or neutered and has no recognised obedience certificate.
Training	$200	A short course of private training and annual membership of an obedience club.
Dog walking	$1000	$20 for someone to walk the dog on one day of the week when the family was not able to do this.
Total	**$3422**	

* Note that health insurance is available for dogs – talk to your vet about the provider/s that he or she recommends.

Will you take your dog on holidays?

Holidays

1   Will you take your dog with you on holiday?
2   What effect will this have on the types of holiday that you can take? For example, dogs are not allowed in places such as National Parks and at some beaches, particularly during the summer. Will this suit you?
3   If you will not be taking your dog on holiday, who will look after it for you? Do you have a friend who can take care of it or will you need a kennel service?

After you have considered all of these factors, you should be in a position to answer the following questions:

◆   Can we look after a dog?
◆   Is a dog the best pet for our family?
◆   What sort of characteristics are we looking for in a dog?

If you decide a dog is right for your family, the information and guidelines in Chapter 7 will help you choose the best type of dog for you.

We recommend you choose to get a puppy rather than an older dog so that you can socialise it properly (see Chapter 10). If you decide to get an older dog, have an experienced person, preferably a dog trainer, assess the dog's response to children before introducing it into the family.

Chapter 3

Kids and dogs are great together and often develop extremely fulfilling relationships with minimal involvement from parents. In most cases, a few simple measures will allow you to sit back and let the natural bond between them work its magic. To help the relationship along, we use some established principles of human and animal behaviour which have been studied and developed by psychologists. Essentially, we use the technique of positive reinforcement to shape behaviour – it works with both kids and dogs. The Lessons section of this book includes an example of how to explain this technique to children, while the principles are explained more fully for adults and teenagers in this chapter.

The psychology of kids and dogs

Operant conditioning

Operant conditioning is one of the most powerful techniques that can be used to shape the behaviour of children. This is also the principle on which the Gentle Modern Method of Dog Training™ is based. Operant conditioning is the process of rewarding or 'reinforcing' a behaviour to increase the likelihood that the behaviour will occur again. You can use positive or negative reinforcement.

Positive reinforcement involves the presentation of something pleasant to increase the likelihood that the behaviour will occur again. For instance, if a child receives a gold star for neat writing, this increases the likelihood that the child will try hard to write neatly in future. In this example the behaviour is writing, and the reinforcer is the gold star.

Negative reinforcement refers to the removal of something unpleasant to increase the likelihood that the behaviour will occur again. Negative reinforcement is rarely used to teach humans but is common in the type of dog training that utilises choker chains. Negative reinforcement *must* be preceded by either a punishment or a threat of punishment. Punishment too may be *positive* or *negative*.

Positive punishment refers to the use of an unpleasant action to decrease the likelihood that an undesirable behaviour will occur; an example is smacking a child. In dog training, jerking a dog on the neck with a choker chain is a positive punishment designed to stop the dog pulling. When the dog stops pulling, the choker chain goes slack, removing the pain and pressure on the neck. This is negative reinforcement – it removes something unpleasant (pain) and thus increases the likelihood of the dog walking without pulling in the future.

Negative punishment refers to the withdrawal of something desirable to decrease the likelihood that an undesirable behaviour will occur; an example is withdrawing TV privileges for children or withdrawing social attention for dogs.

Logically it is always much more efficient, enjoyable and humane to show a child or dog what you expect them to do and then positively reinforce their behaviour, than to wait for the child or dog to make an error in order to teach them by using punishment and negative reinforcement. Punishment also has numerous negative consequences such as creating fear and affecting a child's, or dog's, ability to learn.

Primary and secondary reinforcers

Human and animal behaviour can often be put down to the effects of operant conditioning. However, unlike other animals, much of human behaviour in Western societies is the result of *secondary* reinforcers such as money, appreciation and praise. Animals respond mainly to *primary* reinforcers such as food but also to secondary reinforcers such as praise. Primary reinforcers are classified as those that have an immediate biological importance and are essential to survival, such as food, water and sex. In developed countries, most people have more than enough food and water to survive and hence secondary reinforcers take on more value.

Many reinforcers have individual relevance – what constitutes a reinforcement for one individual may not be a reinforcement for another. However, some reinforcers are universally valued. One of the most powerful universal reinforcers is praise. Praise has an intrinsic value. That is, we value it for what it offers us, not because we can trade

---

Two types of reinforcement and two types of punishment

Reinforcement (positive or negative) **increases** the likelihood that a certain behaviour will occur in the future. **Punishment** (positive or negative) **decreases** the likelihood that a certain behaviour will occur in the future. The terms **positive** and **negative** refer to whether your actions involve **presenting something good** (for example, praise for children, food for a dog) or **removing something bad** (for example, stopping smacking a child or slackening the dog's choker chain).

it for something else. It affirms that we have done something well and makes us feel confident about trying to achieve further goals. Praise from parents, siblings and friends is a particularly effective method of shaping the behaviour of children and can be used to help your child interact positively with the family dog.

Shaping

Positive reinforcement relies on the person or animal behaving the way you wish, before you can reinforce their behaviour. This raises the issue of what to do if the desirable behaviour never occurs. This is where shaping comes in. Shaping is a technique in which successive approximations to the desired behaviour are reinforced until the desired behaviour is achieved. For example, if your daughter is responsible for taking your dog for long walks but refuses to do so, you need to wait until she does something similar, even if it's not exactly what you want, and reinforce that instead. In this case, you may need to wait until your child takes the dog for a short walk or even throws the ball for the dog, and then immediately reinforce the child's behaviour. The reinforcement may be a positive comment like, 'Brook really seems to enjoy it when you take her for a bit of a walk or give her some exercise'.

Shaping can also be used to overcome children's fear or anxiety in the presence of a dog. If your child is afraid to go near the dog, you can reinforce her for just being in the room with the dog. Once she

Shaping can be used to encourage positive interaction

becomes accustomed to that, you can reinforce her for moving closer to the dog and eventually touching it. It is important in this situation that the dog remains calm (lying peacefully or perhaps even sleeping if the child is very nervous) so that the child feels comfortable and safe at all times when the dog is present.

Shaping is also useful for helping your child to learn how to train the dog. For instance, your son may practise a certain hand signal but not get it quite right. To begin with you would praise him for a hand signal that moved in the right sort of direction and then praise successive attempts that got closer and closer to the perfect signal. (Note that it's best to practise without the dog in this situation so that you don't confuse it.)

A few more facts about reinforcers

◆ Reinforcers such as praise are most effective when they immediately follow the behaviour that you wish to reward.

◆ Intermittent reinforcement produces longer lasting behaviours than continuous reinforcement.

◆ Ignoring behaviour tends to extinguish it. Sometimes parents ignore children when they behave well (for example, feed the dog) but respond when they behave badly (for example, forget to feed the dog). Unfortunately we are all guilty of this at times! This has the effect of rewarding the bad behaviour by giving the child attention and discouraging the desired behaviour by ignoring it. We tend to do the same thing with dogs, for example, by paying attention to them when they bark or scratch on the door and ignoring them when they are lying quietly.

What does this mean for teaching your child to help look after your dog?

1   Reinforce desired behaviours immediately after they occur. It is also useful to explain to your children *why* it is good that they perform a certain behaviour. For instance, if it is your daughter's job to groom your pet you may say, 'You did a great job of grooming Brook today, her coat looks so shiny!' Or if it is her responsibility to ensure that your dog always has fresh water you might say, 'Thanks for always making sure Brook has water. It is great for me to know I can rely on you and don't have to worry about it myself.'

2   The reinforcer does not need to be provided every time the behaviour occurs; in fact it is best *not* to reinforce a behaviour constantly. Knowing when and when not to reward your children can be difficult. To some extent you will need to take your cues from them. If your son appears to be tiring of certain activities, it may be a sign that you are not providing sufficient reward. As well as praise for a job well done, children also appreciate the occasional material reward – maybe a gift with a thank-you card, or a special outing.

3   The exception to the rule of only rewarding behaviour intermittently is if you give pocket money. If you promise to give your child a certain sum of money for performing certain tasks then you need to do so consistently. The reinforcing power of pocket money can be increased by reminding children how they earned the money. ('Here is your pocket money for the week, you have done a great job of grooming Brook.')

If your children help out without being asked, it is important to take notice and say thanks. Remember not to take them for granted – children don't like this any more than adults do!

4   If your older child forgets to do their bit in caring for the family dog, but this happens infrequently, it is best not to make a big deal out of it. Keep in mind that we all get busy, tired and forgetful, and that none of us are immune from slipping up from time to time. Try drawing attention to the issue in a way that illustrates understanding rather than criticism. For instance, you may comment, 'You must have been busy this week – I noticed you haven't had time to groom Brook. Would you like me to do it for you or will have you time in the next few days?' Most children will respond positively to this type of comment and try to get the grooming done when they can. If they are too busy then your offer to help will make them feel supported rather than that they have failed. Even if you have to do things yourself from time to time, in the long term, children are much more likely to behave responsibly when they are treated with respect and understanding rather than with criticism. Offering to help your children with their tasks if they are tired or busy also models good behaviour and teaches them to do the same when *you* need a bit of help.

Watching out for overjustification

As discussed above, positive reinforcement can increase the likelihood of producing desirable behaviour. However, while this principle pretty much always works when training your dog, there are some circumstances under which it may not work for children. Sometimes when a child engages in a task or activity because she enjoys it, rewarding this behaviour can actually lead to a decline in the activity.

In a famous experiment conducted in the 1970s, one group of pre-school children were given certificates as a reward for drawing pictures with felt-tipped pens while another group received no reward. In the short term, this had the effect of leading the first group to spend more time engaging in this activity than those who were not rewarded with the certificates. However, when the certificates were no longer given out, those children who had previously received the reward showed a marked decline in their use of the felt-tipped pens, to a level well below that of the children who were never rewarded. This decline in a behaviour is called the 'overjustication effect', because the reinforcer provides an unnecessary justification for engaging in what was already an enjoyable activity.

In these situations, the child (or adult) comes to see the activity as work rather than play. Work is something that is done, at least in part, for an external reward, whereas play is something that is done for the intrinsic value it provides. This is not to say that work does not provide intrinsic value as well – many of us get significant satisfaction from our work – just that play is all about pure fun, while work may involve doing some things that we don't particularly like in order to achieve an external reward.

Dogs offer unconditional love and companionship

The main lesson that we learn from these sorts of experiments is that children do not always need to be reinforced for engaging in activities that are already rewarding and pleasurable in themselves. This is particularly relevant to looking after the family dog, since a lot of children enjoy doing it, and because it is an activity that we *want* children to view as play rather than work. Children receive a multitude of intrinsic rewards, such as unconditional love and companionship, from developing a relationship with the family dog.

The best way to avoid the overjustification effect is not to give children material rewards for doing things they already appear to enjoy. Knowing when to reinforce your child and what reinforcer to provide can be a tricky business and requires some judgement on your part. Some rules of thumb are:

◆ Determine what sort of activities your children like doing with your dog and allow them to take some responsibility for these things (for example, walking, grooming, training).

◆ Don't give children material rewards (such as money or toys) for engaging in these enjoyable activities – the intrinsic reward is enough.

Some activities are intrinsically rewarding for children and dogs!

- Use praise instead – children always enjoy being told that they are doing something well.
- Try to focus your praise on what the child is doing as well as what the dog is doing (for example, 'You're becoming a very proficient dog trainer. Brook is getting good at sitting and staying' or 'Brook looks great – it must be your weekly grooming that keeps her looking so well').

Classical conditioning

Classical conditioning occurs when one stimulus comes to be associated with another because they tend to occur at the same time. The most well known example of classical conditioning is that of Pavlov's dogs. Ivan Pavlov discovered this process almost by accident when he was studying digestion in dogs. Pavlov already knew that dogs salivated when food was placed in their mouths – this is a reflex response. Over time, he noticed that the dogs began to salivate *before* they received the food. He came to realise that certain signals (for example, the sound of the food being prepared) alerted the dogs to the fact that they were about to be fed and caused them to salivate. To study this further, Pavlov began to introduce other stimuli, such as ringing a bell, before he fed the dogs. To his surprise, he noticed that soon the bell alone was enough to make the dogs salivate; no food was necessary. Pavlov called this response a *conditioned* response.

When considering the importance of classical conditioning in building a good relationship between your child and dog, it is important to realise that *emotional* responses can become classically conditioned to occur in certain situations. For instance, if parents complain and argue about the dog whenever it is around, then the children may develop a negative association between the presence of the dog and feeling upset. Similarly if parents focus all of their attention on the dog when going for a walk, children may associate the dog with feelings of being ignored and left out. By the same token, if parents devote all of their attention to the children and ignore the dog, the dog may develop an association between the presence of the children and feeling left out. This is particularly important to remember if you bring a new baby home (see Chapter 8).

To avoid these problems, parents need to ensure that children and dogs develop positive feelings about each other. This can be done by creating pleasant environments where both your child and your dog associate each other with feeling valued and having fun. Encourage your child to take on the responsibility of helping to look after the dog by doing something that they both enjoy (such as walking, feeding, grooming or training). Encourage your

Dogs and kids should have fun together

child to play with the dog by throwing a ball or dumbbell or by teaching it to catch. Perhaps give your child some money to buy the dog a new toy.

Expectations

To some extent, we all act in a manner consistent with how others expect us to behave – this is known as a self-fulfilling prophecy. In one well-known experiment, researchers led primary school teachers to believe that certain students would show a spurt in intellectual growth during the following months, as indicated by a special test that all students had taken. In fact, the students labelled as 'spurters' had been selected randomly and not on the basis of any test score. Despite this, when the children were tested eight months later, the selected 'spurter' students showed significantly improved IQ test results and academic performance compared to the children who were not selected.

This result is thought to relate to the behaviour of the teacher. Many subsequent research studies have found that when teachers expect a certain child to perform well they treat that child differently from the others. Teachers are more likely to praise these children for doing something well, take the time to answer their questions, chat with them, provide them with challenging work, and praise them for showing initiative. In response to the teachers' behaviour, children develop a view of themselves as capable, competent and good students, so work harder and achieve more.

Like the teachers in this experiment, parents who expect a certain level of performance from their children can significantly influence their children's competence and therefore self-esteem. For instance, if parents believe, and act as if their son is capable of feeding the dog every day, then he is more likely to do this effectively. If parents act as if this task is difficult for the child, for example, by supervising him too closely, continually asking if he needs assistance or doing it themselves before he has had sufficient opportunity, then the child is less likely to become proficient at the task. Children tend to look to their parents for clues about how to see themselves and interpret high parental expectations as evidence of their parents' faith in their ability.

Other experiments have shown that when children are made aware that a certain positive trait has been attributed to them, their behaviour becomes consistent with that trait. In one experiment, some children were told that they *were neat and tidy*, others were told that they *should be neat and tidy*, and still others were given *no special message about neatness and tidiness*. As you may have guessed, the result was that those who were told they *were* neat and tidy showed significant improvements in neatness compared to the children in the other categories. Similarly, in another experiment, children who were told that they *were* good at maths showed greater increases in maths test scores than children who were told that they *should try to become* good at maths.

This result can be explained in terms of self-concept. When a child is given some positive information about herself, she incorporates the information into her view of herself and then makes sure it remains true.

You may be wondering if you have to lie to use this technique. Well, the short answer is no! It is not useful to say something to your child that is obviously untrue, because children are remarkably perceptive and they will probably know that you are not being honest with them. The better approach is to wait until your child does something even *pretty well* and then tell her she is good at it. For example, if she becomes involved in training the dog,

Give your child plenty of positive feedback

it is a good idea to tell her that she is doing a good job early on in the process. Just wait until the dog starts learning *something* and then tell the child that she is a good dog trainer. When making these sorts of statements, it is best if they:

- are positive
- are phrased in the present tense
- include the child's name.

For example, 'You're a great dog trainer, Kelly. Brook has learned so much already'. This will help your child incorporate 'good dog trainer' into her self-image and will give her the confidence to keep at the activity. This strategy also helps your child to cope with setbacks, as she is more likely to view the setback as a temporary problem rather than the result of her inability to train. After all, she is a good dog trainer – everybody says so!

Modelling

People learn by watching others and imitating their behaviour. This is particularly true of children. Children don't just learn physical skills (such as using a knife and fork or cooking a meal) by observation, but also how to behave in certain social situations. In a famous experiment conducted by the psychologist Albert Bandura in the late 1960s, one group of children observed an adult behaving very aggressively towards a large inflated doll. The adult yelled abuse at the doll, hit it, kicked it and threw objects at it. A second group of children watched the adult interact gently with the doll, and a third group of children were not shown any adult model at all. Some time later, the children were put in the same room and were allowed to play with any of the toys available, including the inflated doll. The children in the first group behaved the most aggressively towards the doll, performing the same aggressive actions as the adult and also making up some new aggressive behaviours which were directed at not just the doll but also many of the other toys. These results indicate that the children in this group copied specific types of aggression (hitting, kicking, verbal abuse) directly from the adult model and also generalised from these behaviours to learn that aggression in that particular environment was acceptable.

We've probably all heard of situations where an adult who was abused as a child starts to abuse their own offspring. This is a complex issue, but modelling certainly plays a role in passing the behaviours from parent to child. Incidentally, the same notion applies to dogs: dogs that are treated aggressively will behave aggressively. This is just one reason why it is so important to encourage your children to use positive reinforcement with your dog and never punishment techniques such as the use of correction chains.

Kids learn gentle behaviour from others

The other major finding from Bandura's study was that the children who had observed the adult behaving gently with the doll demonstrated less aggressive behaviour than both of the other groups of children. The important message here in terms of kids and dogs is that children will model not only aggressive behaviour but also gentle behaviour, such as patting a dog and caring for it by feeding and exercising it.

Exceptions to the rule

Use of operant and classical conditioning, high parental expectations and modelling can be remarkably powerful tools. When applied consistently these techniques can be enormously effective in helping to establish a positive relationship between your child and dog. However, it would be naive to think that things will always go exactly to plan. Occasionally problems will arise and you will need other strategies for managing these problems. It is in this context that we describe punishment and the use of a token economy.

Punishment

You cannot teach a new behaviour using punishment unless an undesirable behaviour has occured first. Punishment is never as successful as positive reinforcement in shaping a child's behaviour. It can also have negative consequences. For example, if a mother scolds her daughter when she forgets to feed the dog, the scolding elicits negative emotional responses such as fear, anger or hurt in the child.

◆ If the punishment occurs frequently, any stimuli present during the punishment (through classical conditioning) may become conditioned stimuli for negative emotions. This can include the mother herself (the daughter begins to associate her mother with feelings of fear, anger or hurt) or the dog (the child begins to associate the dog with being scolded and develops negative feelings towards the animal).

◆ Through observational learning, the mother's scolding may teach the child to use this method to control the behaviour of others. This may include the use of punishment to control the behaviour of the dog, but could also be generalised to others. For instance, children who are punished a lot during childhood are more likely to use punishment to control the behaviour of adults and their own children later in life.

Having said this, it may be necessary to punish children as a last resort, provided they are capable of understanding why they are being punished. Punishment might be necessary to stop a particularly harmful behaviour that puts the child – or anyone else – at risk. For example, if a child constantly provokes the neighbour's dog in such a way as to make the dog behave aggressively, it could end in a serious injury.

There are several ways to make punishment more effective and ensure it is not detrimental to the child. Punishment works best if it is accompanied by an explanation of why it is being applied. A short explanation is most effective, as the child is more likely to remember the key message. Punishment should also be applied consistently on every occasion that the undesirable behaviour occurs. It should be applied in an atmosphere of love and trust, not an atmosphere of hostility.

We recommend you avoid physical punishment at all times. Physical punishment such as smacking can teach the child to use aggression in dealing with animals and other people. Repeated or erratic use of physical punishment can lead to the child feeling unable to control his own life. He may develop feelings of helplessness and become passive. Children may also attempt to avoid their parents, which decreases the parents' ability to influence the child.

An example of effectively used punishment might be in the situation mentioned earlier, where your son repeatedly provokes the neighbour's dog. You try to help him understand why this is dangerous by discussing the likely consequences. You ask: 'How do you think the dog feels when you tease him?' 'What might the dog do if he feels afraid or hurt?' You explain: 'When you tease the dog it makes him afraid and hurts him. When he feels afraid and hurt he might bite you to protect himself. We love you and are worried that you may be bitten.' If all this fails, an effective punishment would be to tell the

Physical punishment, punishment that is applied in an atmosphere of hostility, or punishment that is applied erratically can be harmful to your child. Likewise, physical punishment should never be used on dogs. Dogs don't have the ability to understand the concept of 'right' and 'wrong', or putting themselves at risk. Using punishment can also adversely affect their temperament.

child to go home immediately instead of staying to play at the neighbour's house.

A token economy

It would be nice if your child loved grooming the dog every week and this behaviour never needed to be reinforced except with the occasional positive comment. However, there are times when children *do* see caring for the dog as a chore and when it is difficult to get them to do it. If this happens you need to decide whether or not to make your child perform the task. Clearly children sometimes need to do things they don't particularly enjoy. However, it's not generally advisable to force a child to help care for your dog if they really dislike doing it as it may lead to feelings of resentment towards the dog. Where possible try to find a way for the child to participate by doing something enjoyable.

If you do need to modify your child's behaviour, a token economy system may be useful when the other methods discussed in this book have been tried but are not working effectively. In this system, the child is rewarded with a token, which can be saved and cashed in later for something desirable. The tokens may be actual tokens or just points that are listed on a board or the fridge. The child works to obtain certain rewards (for example, going to the movies) by accumulating a certain number of tokens. This type of system is often used to assist children with behavioural problems. It can be helpful as it offers a very structured approach that eliminates any delay between good behaviour and a reward. If your child does have behavioural problems and you would like to implement this type of system, we recommend that you seek professional help.

Chapter 4

Many animals, including humans, communicate using body language, but to dogs body language is particularly important. All breeds of dog are descended from wolves, whether they are a tiny chihuahua or an enormous Great Dane. Wolves are naturally social creatures, preferring to live in packs where they communicate by smell and body language, and dogs have inherited these characteristics. It is important to teach children to understand this language for their own safety if nothing else.

The confident, friendly dog

Friendly dogs look generally relaxed. The hair lies flat on the body and the tail usually flags from side to side at about half mast, except when they are concentrating on something really interesting, when the tail tends to hang straight down. The ears will generally be erect and the teeth will not be exposed.

Confident, friendly dog

Reading a dog's body language

The aggressive dog

As a rough guide, bold and aggressive dogs make themselves look bigger and more imposing. The idea is to bluff an opponent into backing down without actual physical confrontation. The dog stands tall with the tail and the hair along its back erect. It stares at its adversary in a very direct manner. If it is particularly intent, the end of the tail starts to vibrate. Some children could think the wagging tail means the dog is friendly – not so! The ears are erect and the lips are sometimes pulled back to show the teeth. Most people will recognise the threat of this type of posture, although it can be difficult to interpret the intentions of some breeds: for example, the hair on Samoyeds, Siberian huskies and malamutes always looks erect.

Nervous dog

The nervous dog

A nervous or subordinate dog will generally make itself appear smaller in an attempt to appease an opponent and look less threatening. The body is usually lowered towards the ground and the tail is tucked under the body. The ears go down and point backwards, or they may be completely flattened onto the head. If cornered, this type of dog may lunge forward and bite, then retreat. Some nervous dogs may roll over to expose their belly area, much as a puppy would do to its mother.

How to approach a friendly dog

Kids should be taught not to run up to any dog to pat it, whether it appears friendly or not. This is particularly important if they don't know the dog. They should ask the dog handler whether they may stroke the dog and, if permission is given, approach the dog from a front-side angle so it can see them coming. It is important not to approach from the rear.

Teach your child to pat a dog under its chin or on its chest rather than on the top of its head. Dominant dogs tend to use standover tactics, and a hand coming over the dog's head may be interpreted as a threatening gesture and could produce an aggressive reaction.

How children (and adults) should respond to a threatening dog or dog attack is covered in the next chapter.

Approaching a dog

With all the news reports of dog bites to kids, it is natural that many parents feel concerned for the safety of their children. However, misconceptions about dog bites are common. It is important that parents understand what causes a dog to bite a child, as lack of guidance from parents on how to interact with dogs is a major factor contributing to dog-bite injuries. The good news though, is that the risk of dog bites can be drastically reduced by training children to read a dog's body language (see Chapter 4), and teaching them appropriate behaviour around dogs.

See if you can identify the following statements about dog bites as true or false.

Children are more likely to be bitten by a strange dog than one they know.
False: Over two-thirds of dog bites are inflicted by dogs known to the child.

Dog bites usually occur when children are walking the streets or playing in the park.
False: 32% of dog bites occur at the child's own home and a further 34% occur at friends' homes.

Only certain breeds of dogs bite.
False: While some dog breeds tend to be more aggressive than others, any dog, if provoked, hurt or frightened, may bite a child. The likelihood that a dog will bite depends on several factors as well as breed, including how they have been socialised and trained, past experiences and treatment by humans, and the behaviour of the child. This chapter discusses how to minimise risk by altering the behaviour of the child, and Chapter 7 gives advice about choosing the type of dog that is suitable for your family.

Chapter 5

Avoiding dog bites

Male dogs are more likely to bite than female dogs.

True: Unneutered male dogs are involved in about three-quarters of reported dog-bite incidents. Unneutered males also represent the majority of dogs brought to dog trainers and veterinarians for problems with dominance aggression, the most commonly diagnosed type of aggression. (Incidentally, in Ruth's experience dominance aggression is often mis-diagnosed by dog handlers. More often dogs react *fearfully* because they have not been adequately socialised or they do not understand what the handler wants them to do.)

However, owning an unspayed female can also be a risk factor for dog bites since females in season tend to attract male dogs. Having unfamiliar male dogs around, especially in the absence of their handlers, increases the risk of dog bites. Female dogs that are not part of a planned breeding program should be spayed before they have their first season, usually by six months of age.

Children are more at risk of dog bites than adults.

True: Almost half of those bitten by a dog are under twelve years old. Active young boys and pre-schoolers are particularly vulnerable. Children's natural behaviours, including quick movements, yelling, screaming, running, jumping, grabbing, hitting and maintaining eye contact, put them at increased risk for dog-bite injuries.

In addition, children have a different smell to adults so dogs may react to them as subordinates. Dogs are pack animals accustomed to operating within a strict hierarchy. In the case of a family, the dog may see itself as being higher up in the pecking order than a young child or baby. This means that the dog may communicate with the child in the same way it would communicate with a dog below it in the hierarchy, by mouthing and potentially biting.

Children are most likely to be bitten on the arm or leg.

False: 51% of dog-bite injuries to children under fifteen are to the face and scalp. A child's relative size and the proximity of a child's face to the dog increases the likelihood of facial injuries.

Dogs not accustomed to small children are more likely to bite.

True: Dogs that are not raised around small children may not have been socialised towards them. These dogs are not accustomed to the way children naturally behave and are more likely to be fearful of them, which increases the likelihood of aggression towards the child.

As this information shows, children are at a disproportionate risk of being bitten by dogs, and when a bite occurs, injuries are most often to the facial area. A dog bite may also cause your child to have a long-term fear of dogs and possibly other animals. A frightened child may behave like a victim, for example, screaming when he sees a dog, which increases the risk of bites in the future. However, the fact that most bites occur in the home or neighbourhood by dogs that are known to the child means that parents can do a lot to prevent dog bites. As a parent, you should always model the correct behaviour around dogs, to serve as an example to your own kids and to other adults.

How to avoid being bitten

◆ Always supervise children under five years of age in the presence of a dog.
◆ Teach your children how to read a dog's body language (see Chapter 4).
◆ Show your children how to approach a dog (see Chapter 4).

- Teach children what to do if they are threatened by a dog (see page 43).
- Choose a type of dog that is suitable to your environment, lifestyle and your child's age (see Chapter 7).
- Socialise your dog and ensure that it has the opportunity to mix safely with children (see Chapter 10).
- Ensure your dog is under your control by properly training it in at least the basics of coming when called, sitting, dropping and staying (see the lessons).
- Train your dog using positive reinforcement. Using compulsive techniques such as choker chains will tend to make dogs more aggressive.
- Encourage your children not to pick up the dog, as this can hurt both dog and child.
- Never play games like tug of war with the more powerful types of dogs such as Rottweilers, as this reinforces aggressive behaviour and makes them more likely to bite in future.
- Never playfight with any dog, especially not by boxing them around the face and mouth.
- Never tease dogs, handle them roughly or hit them.
- Remove your dog from situations where it might become overexcited, such as children's birthday parties.
- Keep a close eye on children visiting your home. They may not be as knowledgeable about how to behave around dogs as your own children.
- Keep the kids away from a sick dog so it can recover in peace.
- Condition your dog to accept people being close to its food dish – preferably when it is a young puppy.
- Avoid cornering a dog, as this can induce fear and fear-related aggression.

- Provide the dog with a quiet bed that is away from high-activity areas.
- Never wake a dog suddenly.
- Don't cuddle a dog face-to-face or grab it around the neck.
- Don't interfere with a mother's new litter of puppies, especially in the first couple of weeks and when her pups are feeding.
- Don't try to take prized possessions away from a dog.

Don't try to take prized possessions away from a dog

How to behave around a strange dog

- Always ask the owner before patting a strange dog.
- Don't play with a strange dog unless the owner is watching.
- Don't bang or climb up on fences when you know there is a dog behind them.
- Don't enter a strange dog's yard unless the owner is present.
- Never run away from a strange dog.
- Don't try to pat a dog which is tied up, even if it looks friendly.
- Don't touch a dog with young puppies unless the owner says you can.
- Don't get into a car which has a strange dog in it, even if the dog looks friendly.
- Don't approach a dog which is in the back of a utility vehicle.
- Don't go up to a strange dog when it is eating.
- Avoid declared 'dangerous' dogs (see page 44).

Don't try to pat a dog which is tied up, even if it looks friendly

Don't go up to a strange dog when it is eating

What to do if threatened by a dog

Needless to say it is best to avoid aggressive or fearful dogs in the first place by reading dogs' body language. However, if you or your child is approached by a dog that looks aggressive, there are a number of things that you can do to defuse the situation:

1   Avoid eye contact with the dog.
2   Stay still and keep your hands still at your sides.
3   Keep quiet – don't scream.
4   Don't run away.
5   If you are carrying something, leave the item on the ground before moving away. With any luck the dog will go to investigate it and leave you alone.
6   Sidle away slowly when you have an opportunity and try to get a barrier such as a fence between you and the dog.
7   If a child is threatened by a dog, they should report the incident to an adult.

What to do if attacked by a dog

Practise what to do if attacked by a dog

1   Curl up in a ball face down (to protect the vital organs).

2   Place your hands over the back of your neck (to protect the back of the neck).
3   Try to make yourself look smaller and less threatening.
4   Stay still until the dog loses interest and moves away.

It's a good idea for you and your child to practise how to behave around strange dogs and what to do if threatened or attacked by a dog. It is also useful for children to practise approaching and patting friendly neighbourhood dogs (under your supervision, of course). Role-playing is a particularly useful method of teaching children what to do.

A recent university study found that even if children are taught about interacting with dogs at school they tend not to remember the information two to four months after the course has finished. However a friend of ours who is a government-approved dog training instructor, and who runs programs for children, has found that even young children retain safety techniques well if they practise the activity both at home and at school. Daniela starts her training by having the children role-play with a stuffed dog before taking one of her own dogs into the classroom. This role-playing helps children to understand and remember how they should act. If you practise with your children at home as well, they are more likely to automatically behave appropriately in a critical situation.

Dangerous dogs

Sometimes dogs are declared 'dangerous'. These are dogs that are trained to attack others, or dogs that have caused serious injury to a person or animal through an unprovoked attack. Legislation governing the control of these animals varies from country to country. Often these dogs are required to be put down. Otherwise they have to be identified in some way such as a special collar, and kept on the lead in public at all times. It is extremely unlikely that you will come across an unrestrained dangerous dog but if you do, avoid it and report the incident to your local authority.

Chapter 6

The stages of child development

As they grow, children progress in their cognitive, physical and emotional development, all of which affect how they relate to the family dog. There are many theories of child development, and psychologists differ in their views on the timing and nature of the changes that occur between birth and adulthood. For the purposes of this book we will divide childhood into four stages: infancy and toddlerhood (birth to three years), early childhood (three to six years), middle childhood (six to twelve years), and adolescence (twelve years to adulthood). As children progress through these stages they develop physically (changes in motor and sensory skills), cognitively (changes in the way they think), and socially (changes in the relationship with self and others). This has implications for what age children can understand certain things about their dog, and what sort of responsibility is appropriate for children of different ages. Understanding the stages of child development will also help you judge how old your child should be before she becomes involved in training the dog and how the relationship between the child and dog will change as she grows older.

Infancy and toddlerhood (birth to three years)

As we all know, babies and toddlers rely on their parents to meet all of their needs, including the physical needs for food, warmth, shelter and safety. Children of this age are not capable of caring for themselves, nor are they able to understand the potential dangers of provoking aggression in a dog, or to make any decisions about how best to interact with an animal. Babies and toddlers therefore need constant supervision when in the presence of a dog.

We do not recommend that parents of babies and toddlers get a dog. Ideally, you should wait until your child is at least four. Families often decide to get a puppy rather than a mature dog, and although this in itself is a good decision, babies, toddlers and puppies are not a good combination. The reasons for this are that babies and toddlers:

◆ need *constant* supervision when in the presence of a dog.
◆ are an enormous amount of work, leaving less time to care for a dog, especially a new puppy.

- do not understand that sticking their fingers into the eyes and mouth of a dog can be painful and may incite aggression.
- can be harmed by even a friendly nip from a puppy, especially given their size and the proximity of their face to the dog.
- are often close to floor level, making them more susceptible to picking up infection from dogs. Trying to toilet train a puppy while your children are very young is not a good idea.
- sometimes suck their thumb which could be contaminated with such things as roundworm eggs.
- cannot help care for a dog. Kids get more out of a new puppy when they are a bit older and can play a role in making the decision to get the puppy and in helping to care for it.

With planning, a mature dog will adapt to a new baby

What if I already have a dog, and then decide to have a child?

If you already have a dog, it is likely to be a mature dog that you already have a good relationship with and who is (hopefully!) trained in at least the basics. There are several things you can do to prepare your dog for the imminent arrival of a new baby. See Chapter 8 for a full discussion of these issues.

Early childhood (ages three to six)

During early childhood, children begin to take on some responsibility for caring for themselves. They become more independent and enjoy new challenges and showing initiative. This is the stage when children will become capable of helping to care for the family dog.

It is best to give the child one task so he feels he has an important role in caring for the dog. The most suitable tasks include helping to make sure the dog's water bowl is full or helping with the grooming. With your help, these tasks are manageable, both cognitively and physically, for kids between three and six.

In the case of filling the water bowl, it generally works best if an adult regularly washes the bowl and fills a light plastic jug with water. The child can then use the jug to fill the bowl. Keep the jug within easy reach of the child but not in the fridge, as very cold water is not absorbed as easily into a dog's system. Depending on their age and maturity, some children will be able to take full responsibility for filling the water bowl themselves, whereas others will need assistance from a parent or older sibling. Another task for a child of this age might be grooming – perhaps with a parent's help. Grooming the dog is usually a positive experience for the animal as well, which will encourage the dog to view the child as an important member of the family. Give your child increased responsibility as he develops the ability to manage these tasks independently.

During this early childhood period, children are still cognitively immature and have many illogical (but often highly entertaining!) ideas about their environment. Children at this stage often do not have a good understanding of cause and effect and are not able to imagine the logical result of certain actions, so it is not realistic for them to become involved in training the dog. Understanding the concepts of dog training requires fairly sophisticated thinking. In addition, children of this age often do not have sufficient self-control to keep still and tend to wave their hands around. If they are holding food when doing this, it obviously creates a very tempting distraction for your dog. Three- to six-year-olds also have trouble applying dog-training methods (such as hand and voice signals) in a consistent manner which will confuse the dog and slow down the training process.

3- to 6-year-olds can practise basic lessons with a well-trained dog

However, if you have a dog that is already **well trained**, a child of this age can be taught how to call the dog (Lesson 1) and sit the dog in front of him (Lesson 2). If he can do this he will feel involved in the dog training and have a level of control over the dog. Make sure he calls and sits the dog under supervision to ensure he doesn't undo your previous training.

Behaviour during early childhood is still largely egocentric, which means that children view things from their own point of view. For instance, a child may believe that the sky is blue because it is his favourite colour or that he should not share his toy because his mum bought it for him. This is perfectly normal, but helping your child to understand the needs and feelings of your dog is a useful way to teach him to view things from the perspective of others. Encourage your child to think about his actions and the effect they have on your dog by asking him questions. Questioning allows children to consolidate their ideas and understanding by putting concepts into their own words. It also allows you to determine your child's level of understanding. For example, if your child smacks the dog, the best approach is not to lecture him on being naughty but to ask, 'How would you feel if someone gave you a smack like that?' This question prompts the child to think about how he would feel in a certain situation. Then say, 'How do you think the dog feels when you smack her?' This question prompts the child to look at the situation from the perspective of another. He learns that we can draw conclusions about the feelings of others based on how we would feel in similar circumstances. This is the basis of empathy.

As well as questioning, the use of stories, games and role-plays are other useful ways to convey messages to children of this age. Because they have not generally achieved the level of cognitive development required for abstract thinking, they often consolidate information most effectively through relating to a character in a story, or practising how they would behave in certain situations.

Middle childhood (ages six to twelve)

During the middle childhood stage, children take on additional responsibilities both at school and at home. Children's perceived success at handling these responsibilities contributes to their view of themselves, their self-concept.

According to the famous psychologist Jean Piaget, it is during middle childhood that children begin to think logically. They acquire the concept of cause and effect and can solve problems, as long as those problems are focused on real events (not abstractions) that are occurring in the here and now.

Helping to care for a dog during the middle childhood years can help kids develop a positive view of themselves. Playing a role in looking after a dependent animal will lead to a sense of satisfaction and success. A lot of positive reinforcement and praise from parents is important here, to ensure that children develop a sense of competence and high self-esteem.

In a similar way to younger children, six- to twelve-year-olds can be responsible for one aspect of caring for the family dog. As they move through this stage they will become increasingly capable of taking on the sole responsibility for this task. An appropriate task might be feeding the dog, making sure the dog always has water, or grooming. Children at age six will still require some supervision and may not be able to prepare a dog's meal,

6- to 12-year-olds can take increasing responsibility for dog care

while twelve-year-olds should be capable of undertaking any of these activities independently. If your child is involved in feeding, first train the dog to sit when its meal is placed on the floor (see Lesson 12), then teach the child to maintain this behaviour. Use plastic, not ceramic, food and drink bowls, just in case the bowl is dropped or broken and so that the child can lift them easily.

Children in middle childhood can also take on increased responsibility for training. Many children eight years of age and older are capable of teaching a dog from scratch, although it's best for parents to oversee the training, at least initially. Children of this age can follow the detailed instructions for training provided in Lessons 1 to 12. Children are very good at following step-by-step instructions, and as they tend to be natural in their hand signals, they often make very effective trainers. When difficulties do arise it is usually because they become excited or exasperated and use inconsistent hand signals. They also tend to practise the lessons that are going well (and can overdo these) and ignore the lessons they find more difficult. Parents can help out by giving positive feedback on good hand signals, calling it quits before the child or dog becomes too worked up, and reinforcing the child when a more challenging lesson pays off.

Questioning and role-playing again are useful methods of helping your primary-school-age children learn (see the section on early childhood for a discussion of these methods). These techniques can also help children think about their behaviours and their consequences, to recognise alternative behaviours, and to make choices about how they intend to respond to particular situations in the future. Rules and contracts can also be effective, as long as children help to develop the rules rather than have them imposed. For instance, children may write a list of the top ten rules for responsible dog ownership or the

'Ross family rules for looking after Brook'. It is also critical that the whole family agrees to the rules and adheres to them. There is no point in setting a family rule if you are not going to stick to it yourself. Be realistic: if you allow your dog to lick the dishes in the dishwasher don't include not licking the dishes at the table as a rule!

Self-centred behaviour diminishes during middle childhood, and children increasingly develop the ability to see things from others' points of view. Parents of children with well-developed social skills usually hold their children to high standards. Children are aware that they have some responsibilities in the home and that they are expected to meet these responsibilities. By conveying to your child that he is totally responsible for feeding the dog, you are not only conveying your trust and faith in his ability, but also demonstrating that you care enough for him to establish standards for him to uphold.

In short, parents need to be both democratic and strict, by establishing clear, consistent rules that let children know what is expected of them. A child who breaks a rule should know that he is breaking it and what the likely consequences of this will be. Such predictability in the environment helps children be in control of their lives and feel secure.

Adolescence (ages twelve to adulthood)

During adolescence, children acquire the ability to solve complex, hypothetical problems and think in abstract terms. Children of this age are able to solve problems by considering various possibilities, synthesising evidence in a systematic way, and drawing conclusions. This level of thinking equips a child to understand and apply the principles of dog training and even to teach others the same techniques. In general, adolescents begin to think like adults and can be fully involved in dog training. The exercises in Lessons 1 to 12 are all suitable for children of this age.

Keep in mind though, that adolescents are still children, and they face specific issues during this period of their lives. A major characteristic of adolescence is the search for identity. As part of this process, adolescents usually develop close relationships with their peers and spend less time with the family. It is normal for teenagers to rebel in an attempt to push the boundaries and establish their independence! An adolescent needs to feel she is a unique person who, on her own, can contribute to society. Although this desire for a unique identity and independence is strong, many adolescents experience conflict in their need to establish themselves and the realisation of how dependent they are on their parents and how much they still need their family.

Teenagers are capable of teaching others

Parents also experience the conflicting desires of letting their children go and yet wanting to keep them close. Many of us realise that this conflict can result in inconsistent or contradictory parental communication!

Changes during adolescence have implications for your child's relationship with the family dog. Arguing over chores is quite common during adolescence, and your child may rebel against her role in caring for your dog. The best approach here is to follow the advice established in Chapter 3 by continuing to set and maintain high standards. It is also critical to be available to listen when your child needs to discuss issues. If your teenager wants less involvement in family life, accept that this is normal and be prepared to negotiate. Children in late high school are particularly busy and may have less time to help care for the dog. However, they need to be clear that you still expect them to play a role in family life.

Many parents become concerned that their teenagers reject parental views and values and are overly influenced by peer pressure. In fact, this is usually a lot less dramatic than it may seem, and adolescents continue to be highly influenced by their parents. Any rebellion is usually temporary and minor.

The characteristics of each age group in a nutshell

0–3 years
- *The acquisition of a new dog is not recommended.*
- *Constant supervision is required if you already have a dog.*

3–6 years
- *Children can start to take some responsibility for one simple task such as helping to groom the dog or fill its water bowl.*
- *They can practise simple lessons such as come when called (Lesson 1) and sit in front (Lesson 2) with a well-trained dog.*
- *Constant parental supervision is required.*

6–12 years
- *Children have the capacity to take increasing responsibility for one or more tasks such as grooming or feeding.*
- *Kids of eight and over are capable of teaching the dog from scratch. The most important lessons for kids to practise are come when called, stay and heel.*

12 years +
- *Adolescents are capable of understanding and applying all principles of dog training.*
- *They can also teach other people about dog training techniques.*
- *The most critical exercises to practise are the same as those for kids six to twelve years.*

Chapter 7

The ideal time to get a dog is when it is seven to eight weeks old. At this age the puppy will readily adapt to a new home and learn to fit into your family (provided you teach it the ground rules – see Chapter 10 on socialisation). It is wise to plan well ahead before buying a dog, as it is going to be part of your family for up to sixteen years. You don't want to give your children the message that animals are disposable items if you find the dog doesn't fit into your family life.

Do your homework first by researching the breed of dog you feel would suit your lifestyle – we discuss the issues later in this chapter. If you intend to get a crossbred or mongrel dog, make sure it is structurally sound and you know the temperament and genetic propensity of both parents. If you cannot see both parents, consider getting a purebred dog. The parents of a purebred dog should have been genetically screened for the inherited problems that are common in that breed. You might like to go to a puppy school or a dog show to see how various

Puppy school

The right

dog for

your

family

types of dogs behave. Purebred dogs cost a lot more initially but it is often more economical to pay more for a puppy that has been carefully bred and has had a good start in life, both nutritionally and socially, than to decide to take on a dog because it is inexpensive or free. We see a lot of dogs that require expensive surgery to correct skeletal problems. Worse still, we see the heartbreak when a young dog dies or is put down prematurely due to medical or temperament problems related to inappropriate breeding.

Whether you get a male or female dog is largely a question of choice. Males tend to grow a bit bigger and heavier and can sometimes be more aggressive towards other male dogs. They also have a greater tendency to roam if they are not castrated. Statistically, male dogs that are not castrated end up in shelters more often than females or desexed males. Males scent mark more by urinating on upright objects – some people don't like this! But if you have energetic teenagers, a robust male dog may suit them well. Females tend to be more gentle and are more suitable for young children.

How and where should I purchase my puppy?

The best place to buy a purebred puppy is from a professional breeder, especially if you want it to be registered so that you can show it or take part in official obedience trials. The canine association in your area will have details of the breed clubs, and the clubs themselves nearly always keep a list of responsible breeders. You can also ask around and seek recommendations from people who have gone through the process. Check that the breeder will let you have the dog at eight weeks of age before you go any further. Some breeders like to keep their puppies until they are older to choose the best one for themselves. You will be behind the eight ball if you agree to this.

Make appointments to go and look at litters of puppies. It will help if you have decided whether you want a male or female before you go – looking at a large litter can become a bit confusing. Some puppies are naturally bold and some are shy. Others are middle of the road temperamentally, which is possibly more suitable for a family with children. Expect the breeder to ask *you* questions as well. Are you going to be a responsible dog owner? Is the dog going to suit your lifestyle? Be guided by the breeder's advice, particularly if you have a child with special needs.

Pet shops and shelters may seem an easy place to find a puppy, but they're not the best option, particularly when you're looking for a family dog. Pet shops may or may not have the type of dog you want. They are also a magnet for children and likely to lead to a decision based on heart, not head. Impulse buying may result in much heartache later if the dog turns out to be sick, too large or aggressive. If you decide to get your dog from a pet shop, choose a shop in your neighbourhood that has a good reputation.

Shelters do a great job and we admire the people who work in them very much. But remember it is important to get your dog at the right age and with a suitable temperament. Shelter staff rarely know the background of the dogs who end up there. Who knows if there has been a problem with children in the past? Some shelters are better at assessing the dog's temperament than others. If you feel unsure about adopting a shelter dog it is better to play it safe and steer clear. You can always make a donation to help the dogs that need to be re-homed.

- *Get your puppy when it's eight weeks old.*
- *Choose a reputable breeder.*
- *Start to socialise and train your puppy from day one.*

Do your homework before choosing a puppy

Which breed?

Choose the breed of dog that will best suit your family according to your children's age and stage of development. In general, small dogs suit families with young children because of their light bodyweight, although many larger dogs are also suitable. Terriers, working dogs and some of the heavier large dogs are less suitable for families with young kids. It is better not to get a dog until your youngest child is at least four years old, particularly if you have never had a dog before. However, if you do decide to get a dog when you have a baby or toddler, follow the guidelines suggested for three- to six-year-olds overleaf.

Kids with special needs

Take extra care when choosing a suitable breed for a child with special needs. The right breed will depend very much on the particular needs of your child. For example, if your child is not physically strong, a smaller dog may be best. If you have any doubts, once again, the breeds listed as suitable for ages three to six are the safest bet.

The tables can be interpreted as follows:

Trainability: This is measured on a scale of 1 to 5, with 1 indicating a breed that is harder to train using our Gentle Modern Method of Training™ and 5 showing the most easily trained breeds. A rating of 3 is average.

Temperament and notes: Comments on the typical temperament of the breed, as well as any other important issues which may influence your decision.

Ages 3–6: Rates the dog's suitability for children of this age (the early childhood period). We advise against most of the terriers for this age group as they tend to be more reactive and aggressive than some other breeds. In fact, small terriers are more likely to nip than larger breeds. We have rated many of the large dogs as unsuitable for this age group because they are strong, heavy and active, not necessarily because they don't have a good temperament. Treat the large guarding breeds and working dogs with extra caution. *Children in this age group should be supervised with dogs at ALL times.*

Ages 6–12: Indicates dogs that are suitable for children of this age (the middle childhood period). Breeds marked with an asterisk may be more easily triggered to react if teased or handled roughly. However, when children are taught to behave appropriately around them these dogs can make wonderful companions. Children of this age should be supervised by an adult or teenager when they take the dog for a walk.

Ages 12 upwards: We regard children over twelve as adults for the purposes of this book.

* An asterisk indicates that children in that age group should be supervised with extra care around the particular breed of dog.

Cairn Terrier

Choose a breed to suit your family

Cavalier King Charles Spaniel

Small breeds

Breed	Trainability	Temperament and notes	Child's age 3–6	6–12	12+
Australian Terrier	3	bold	no	yes*	yes
Basenji	2	determined, doesn't bark	yes	yes	yes
Bassett Hound	2	quiet, prone to disc problems	yes	yes	yes
Beagle	3	sound, distracted by scent	yes	yes	yes
Bedlington Terrier	2	independent	yes	yes	yes
Bichon Frise	3	friendly	yes	yes	yes
Border Terrier	4	bold	yes*	yes*	yes
Cairn Terrier	4	bold	no	yes*	yes
Cavalier King Charles Spaniel	4	friendly	yes	yes	yes
Chihuahua	2	independent	no	yes*	yes
Chinese Crested	2	quiet, suitable if have allergies, can get sunburnt easily	yes	yes	yes
Cocker Spaniel	4	excitable, can be possessive	no	yes*	yes
Corgi	2	feisty	no	yes*	yes
Dachshund	2	feisty, prone to disc problems	no	yes*	yes
Fox Terrier	3	bold	no	yes*	yes
Hungarian Puli	3	bold, corded coat	no	yes	yes
Jack Russell Terrier	4	bold	no	yes*	yes
Lakeland Terrier	3	sound	no	yes	yes
Maltese Terrier	3	sound	yes	yes	yes
Papillon	3	sound, barks	yes	yes	yes
Pekinese	2	quiet	yes	yes	yes
Pomeranian	4	excitable, can be yappy	yes	yes	yes
Poodle (toy)	4	excitable, can be yappy	yes	yes	yes
Pug	4	friendly, can be snuffly	yes	yes	yes

Medium-sized breeds

Breed	Trainability	Temperament and notes	Child's age 3–6	6–12	12+
Border Collie	5	excitable	no	no	yes
Boxer	3	excitable, pushy with other dogs	no	no	yes
Brittany Spaniel	4	sound	yes	yes	yes
Bulldog	2	slow	yes	yes	yes
Bull Terrier	3	strong	not recommended		

Breed	Trainability	Temperament and notes	Child's age 3–6	6–12	12+
Cattle Dog	5	active, can herd and nip	no	no	no
Curly-coated Retriever	4	sound	yes	yes	yes
Dalmatian	4	active	no	yes	yes
German Short-haired Pointer	4	active	no	yes	yes
Golden Retriever	5	sound	yes	yes	yes
Keeshond	3	independent	yes	yes	yes
Kelpie	5	active	no	yes*	yes
Labrador	5	sound, boisterous	no	yes	yes
Samoyed	3	friendly	yes	yes	yes
Schnauzer (standard)	3	can be possessive	no	no	yes
Shetland Sheepdog	4	reserved	yes	yes	yes
Siberian Husky	5	independent	no	no	yes
Spitz	3	independent	yes	yes	yes
Staffordshire Bull Terrier	4	bold, pushy with other dogs	not recommended		
Welsh Springer Spaniel	5	sound	yes	yes	yes
Whippet	2	reserved	yes	yes	yes

Large breeds

Breed	Trainability	Temperament and notes	Child's age 3–6	6–12	12+
Airedale	3	reserved	no	yes*	yes
Alaskan Malamute	3	strong	no	no	no
Bearded Collie	3	active	no	yes*	yes
Bernese Mountain Dog	3	sound	yes	yes	yes
Bull Mastiff	2	sound	no	yes	yes
Collie	4	reserved	yes	yes	yes
Dobermann	3	flighty	no	yes*	yes
Gordon Setter	2	quiet	yes	yes	yes
Greyhound	1	quiet	yes	yes	yes
Irish Setter	2	flighty	yes	yes	yes
Irish Water Spaniel	2	flighty	yes	yes	yes
Newfoundland	4	sound	no	yes	yes
Old English Sheepdog	2	excitable	no	yes	yes
Pointer	3	sound	yes	yes	yes
Poodle (standard)	5	excitable	yes	yes	yes
Rottweiler	5	strong and heavy	no	no	yes*

Labrador

Dalmatian

Right: Bernese Mountain Dog
Far right: Newfoundland

Dog laws

Some governments ban some of the more dangerous breeds of dogs, so check which ones are banned in your area. If you have kids, these are probably not the ones you would want anyway! Laws regulating dog ownership differ from country to country and even among states, territories and local authorities. For example, seventy-four breeds are reportedly banned in Italy while there are plans to stop the *importation* of four breeds in New Zealand: American pitbull terriers, Brazilian filas, Dogo argentinos and Japanese tosas.

The most commonly banned dog in the Western world is the American pitbull terrier type. Others high on the list are American Staffordshire bull terriers, bull terriers and Staffordshire bull terriers. Certain breeds are also required to be desexed and muzzled in public. Needless to say, these types of dogs are not suitable for families.

We don't recommend that you get a puppy or dog if you are planning to have children in the very near future. Babies and puppies both require an enormous amount of attention, and inevitably it is the puppy that is neglected. New parents are understandably often tired and emotional and have enough to cope with without introducing a puppy into the picture. However, if you already have a dog in the family and a new baby is on the way, you will find that with a bit of planning most dogs easily adapt to the new family member.

Our knowledge of wolf behaviour tells us that older wolves nurture young pack members and do not pose a danger to them. The same applies to dogs and babies. Dogs that are part of the family will simply regard the new baby as a young member of the pack.

Dogs should have regular, safe exposure to children throughout their life. If your dog has not had the opportunity to be around children, start to familiarise it with children as soon as possible. This should be done gradually. Begin by taking your dog to a place where children play and allow the dog to walk past the children. Most dogs cope easily with this situation, but if you have any doubts, keep your dog on a lead.

Next arrange to meet some children you know in a neutral area such as a local park. Always introduce your dog to children in an open area and not a confined space such as a small room. Don't introduce a dog to children at the dog's home, where it may defend its territory. Have the child hold out her hand, palm down. Allow the dog to sniff the child. Monitor interactions closely.

If you have any doubt about the ability of your dog to relate to children, seek professional advice. Similarly, if your dog has engaged in an unprovoked attack on a child

Chapter 8

Bringing home a new baby

in the past, or has a history of behavioural problems, have the dog evaluated by a professional before bringing a new baby into the home. In the event that your dog is considered a risk to a new baby, we strongly recommend rehousing the dog. Unfortunately, not all problems can be solved, and it is too risky to have an unsuitable dog in the same home as any child.

Some parents worry that their dog will not be safe around a new baby or that it will spread disease, and therefore feel that the dog should be kept outside while the baby is young. Dogs that are prevented from being part of the family are prone to developing a number of behavioural problems. Jealousy is one reason that a dog may bite a baby, so it is important that the dog continues to feel a part of things and is not left out. Furthermore, the health benefits of a dog to a baby outweigh the risks (see Chapter 11), and with a bit of effort you can ensure that your baby and dog develop a positive, safe relationship that will greatly reward both of them.

Change the dog's routine as little as possible when you bring a baby home. If the dog associates any negative changes with the arrival of the new baby, it will affect their ability to develop a positive relationship. If changes are required (for example, walking the dog less frequently or moving the dog's sleeping place), they should be introduced gradually and well in advance of the baby coming home.

Don't lock your dog away from family life

Make sure the dog is still allowed to play a full role in family life and don't be tempted to lock it out or keep it tied up in the backyard.

Before bringing the baby home, some people find it helpful to practise taking the dog for a walk while also pushing a pram. This enables the dog to become accustomed to walking beside a pram before the baby arrives. Some tips on teaching a dog to heel when you are pushing a pram are included in Lesson 7. It is also helpful to expose the dog to all the new equipment that will be used when the baby comes home (such as cot, clothes, change table). Allow the dog to be around when you are setting up the nursery or place where the baby will sleep. Reinforce the dog for remaining calm in this situation.

Bringing the baby home

When you come home with your new baby, introducing the baby to your dog may be the last thing on your mind. However it only takes a few minutes, has a long-lasting impact on the dog and is well worth the effort.

Introducing your new baby to
your dog

1 Prior to bringing the baby home, 'introduce' the dog to the new baby by allowing it to sniff a piece of the baby's used clothing. This allows the dog to become familiar with the baby's smell in a non-threatening manner.

2 See if a friend can take the dog for a walk immediately before the baby comes home. This will ensure it has had some attention and exercise and will not be feeling restless or excitable.

3 Bring the baby into the house in a carry cot and place the cot on a bed (or something at dog level). Have the dog sit beside the cot and keep its attention focused on you. Reinforce the dog a few times with small bits of its favourite food. This creates a positive association between your dog and the presence (sight and smell) of the baby.

Reinforce your dog for behaving
quietly around the baby

4 Allow the dog to smell and see the baby but not to touch it initially. Monitor all interactions closely. Continue to reinforce the dog with food, praise and patting.

5 When you first pick the baby up in the dog's presence, reinforce the dog with food.

For the first few days after the baby is home, feed the dog only when the baby is in the room. Pat the dog and make a fuss of it when the baby is around. By doing this, the dog comes to associate the baby with lots of great things such as food, attention and pats. Reinforce your dog for behaving quietly around the baby. Place the baby on the floor and get the dog to lie down near it. Stroke the dog and reinforce this quiet behaviour. Remember to keep doing fun things together as a family such as going for a walk or playing in the park.

If you want to put the dog outside, do so before you pick the baby up. Never pick up the baby and then put the dog out, as this creates an association between the baby and feeling left out. Similarly, never scold the dog for picking up one of the baby's toys. It is natural for a dog to want to do this. Teach the dog that this toy does not belong to it by simply removing the toy (wash it thoroughly before returning it to the baby) and replacing it with one of its own. It is best to use preventative strategies by trying to keep the baby's toys out of reach of the dog and ensuring that the dog has enough of its own toys to play with.

Do fun things together

Finally, don't be too hard on yourself if the dog doesn't get quite the amount of attention that it is used to. Enlist the help of other family and friends to walk the dog and hire a dog walker for a few months if you need a hand.

- *Make the dog feel it is still an important part of your family, even when the baby is around.*
- *Reward the dog with food and praise whenever it is behaving well in the baby's presence.*
- *Don't limit your positive interactions with the dog to times when the baby is out of the house or asleep. The dog will come to associate the baby with loss of privileges and feeling left out.*
- *Make sure the dog does not feel replaced by the new baby – continue to give it love, attention and affection.*

As baby grows

As babies grow into toddlers and start to move about, they tend to crawl over the dog and pull at its ears and tail. These situations need to be monitored closely, as it is natural for dogs to bite in response to feeling threatened or hurt. Even dogs that appear extremely tolerant should be monitored, just in case they instinctively lash out in response to pain caused by a toddler.

Child-proof your dog

To minimise the risk of these problems, you can start to 'child proof' your dog while the baby is still young by increasing the dog's tolerance for the types of behaviours that toddlers are likely to engage in. Gently pull the dog's tail and ears, put a toy across its back and gradually increase the weight and pressure. Practise taking food or a bone away from the dog, making loud noises such as screaming, and teaching the dog not to chase things that are moving quickly. Reinforce the dog for reacting appropriately in these situations.

How you behave towards your dog will have a strong effect on the baby. Even from a very young age, babies are influenced by the emotional reactions of others. Right from birth, infants begin to look at their parents or other familiar adults to guide their behaviour. In one experiment, twelve-month-old babies were found to avoid a new toy if their mother showed a facial sign of disgust towards it, but play with it if their mother did not show disgust. If you express fear, stress, disgust or other negative emotions towards the family dog, this can reduce the likelihood that the baby will interact positively

Practise taking food or a bone away from your dog

with the animal. But showing feelings of joy and love towards the dog will facilitate the development of a positive relationship between your baby and dog. Babies from as young as eighteen months of age can form very strong emotional attachments to a dog, so it is important that a positive relationship is encouraged from day one.

Remember, children gain an enormous amount of joy, friendship and fun from having a dog in the family. Most dogs are wonderful companions who love having children around and are surprisingly tolerant. If you follow the simple guidelines above, the relationship between your baby and dog is likely to develop into a lasting and very precious friendship.

Chapter 9

Bringing home a new dog

When you bring a new dog into the family, interactions between family members can change in fairly complex and unpredictable ways. Each person forms a relationship with the new dog, and in many cases this relationship will become a strong and enduring bond. Relationships between family members can also change as they communicate with each other about the dog and sometimes compete for its affection. Feelings between owners and their dogs are strong, so don't be surprised if a new dog inspires envy, jealousy, possessiveness and rivalry in your kids. These feelings are quite normal and nothing to be too concerned about. Think of it as an opportunity for children to learn how to express jealousy and develop strategies for managing this in constructive ways. Sometimes pre-existing tension between siblings is exacerbated by getting a new dog. For instance, one child might feel that her brother always gets to do all the 'fun stuff', so may be annoyed that he shares in training the dog. Another child might feel that his sister is more loved by the family and likewise imagines that the new puppy pays more attention to her than him. Such feelings need to be discussed, and the discussion can help to resolve previously unexplored issues within the family.

As most parents know, children can be very sensitive to feeling left out. If you spend a lot of time doting over the dog, your kids may become jealous, so continue to spend time with them and don't ignore them when the pet is around. Another good strategy is for each family member to be given responsibility for an aspect of caring for the dog, so everyone contributes to nurturing the new family member. Deal with conflicts openly and encourage children to talk about their feelings. After all, most emotional reactions, including jealousy, are normal; it is the way that these emotions are managed that is important.

As always, prevention is better than cure, and rivalry is less likely to occur when there is a clear and well understood sharing of responsibilities. For instance, if you have two children and both want to feed the dog, don't leave the argument to fester. Ask the children how they think the issue could be resolved. Could one of the children take responsibility for another aspect of caring for the dog? Could they alternate responsibility, with one child feeding the dog one night and the other the next? Use this time to teach children some conflict resolution skills and encourage them to work it out. Sibling rivalry is normal and life will always contain some conflict, so learning to deal with these situations is essential.

Preparing to bring the puppy home

Before the puppy arrives, talk to the kids about what will happen. Explain that it is a big move for a puppy to leave its mum and that it will need a lot of care and attention to help it settle in. Give each family member a task to help prepare the home for the arrival of the new puppy, so everyone feels involved. This is also a good time to start teaching the children about responsible dog ownership. Children can help by organising a bed, making a pet menu of what the new family member will eat or a list of dog rules to post on the fridge.

You will need the following equipment when bringing home a new puppy:

◆ A comfortable place for the pup to sleep. Baskets from the pet shop work well, or you can make your own pet bed out of blankets, beanbags or doonas. It's important that the puppy is warm, comfortable and has a place to rest undisturbed. Remember, like babies, puppies need a lot of sleep.

◆ Food and water bowls.

◆ Appropriate food. If possible find out what the breeder has been feeding the pups and get something similar. You can gradually change the diet over time if you wish, but it is not ideal to bring a pup home and dramatically change its diet overnight.

◆ A collar (not choker chain) with identification tag. The nylon ones with a clip rather than eyelets seem to last forever. You may wish to purchase a harness later.

◆ A long, light lead, at least two to three metres in length.

◆ A brush and a comb. (A comb might not be required for short-haired breeds.)

◆ Toys. Again, pet shops have plenty to choose from or you

Pups love their own toys

can make your own or get things from a charity or opportunity shop. Puppies love things that squeak or make a noise and also enjoy things to chew such as pieces of rawhide or brisket bone.

- Secure gates and fences.
- A playpen or dog crate for indoors is very useful.

Teaching the kids how to behave around the puppy

When the new puppy comes home, take care that the children don't inadvertently teach it bad habits, by showing them some basics of how to behave around the puppy.

- Puppies love to mouth and bite. Although this is quite natural, you don't want this behaviour to persist into adulthood. Don't let the puppy bite your children or their clothing. Shoelaces, long hair, hair ribbons, leads and loose clothing are particularly tempting for puppies, so try to keep these out of the way. Teach your children not to run around and get the puppy excited. If the puppy does mouth, the best way to respond is to make a high-pitched squeal. This gives the puppy feedback – 'you're biting too hard' – in language it can understand. Then the child should withdraw social attention from the dog by going away into another room and shutting the door for a minute or so. If you apply this negative punishment technique consistently the puppy should soon get the message: bite and I lose what I want – attention and company. If you give your puppy lots of exercise and give it chews and toys to play with, it will be much less likely to exhibit behavioural problems.

Don't allow your puppy to bite

- Boys in particular sometimes tend to 'play rough' with their puppy, pretending to lunge at it or box with it. This stimulates growling, barking and aggression in the pup. While this is not usually dangerous in a young puppy, the behaviour can carry into adulthood, producing a dog that is more likely to bite. A 'don't play rough' rule is important.
- When children lift their hands to their faces to protect themselves from a jumping or licking puppy, this only encourages the puppy to investigate them further. Children should be taught to remain still and keep their hands quietly at their sides or across their chests.
- Children who scream or shout or flap their hands around trigger excitement in the dogs. Keep them calm!
- Puppies instinctively chase moving objects. This includes children! Teach your children to sit quietly on the floor with the puppy in their lap.

◆ Although a gentle tug of war is a fun game to play with most breeds of dog, never play this game with breeds such as bull terriers, Staffordshire bull terriers, pitbull terrier types or other breeds that tend to hold on to objects and not let go. As soon as possible you should train your puppy to let go of objects and 'give' on signal (see Lesson 9).

If you have another dog in the family

If you have another dog in the family, introduce it to the new dog on neutral ground such as a park before taking them home together. Take them into the garden together first and, when they have settled down, move into the house. Make sure your first dog does not feel left out in all the excitement of bringing the new dog home.

Introduce dogs on neutral ground

How we look after Brook

- *Make sure she has clean water.*
- *Feed her once a day from four months of age onwards.*
- *Make sure she is inside the house with us as much as possible for company.*
- *Ensure she can get outside to the toilet, preferably via a doggy door.*
- *Take her out for a walk at least once a day.*
- *Allow her to socialise with other dogs regularly.*
- *Practise her lessons at home, in the park and lots of different places.*
- *Let her go to her bed and sleep when she is tired and don't wake her up suddenly.*
- *Never tease or hurt her at any time or allow other people do this.*
- *Take her to the vet if she is sick and for her annual immunisation.*
- *Make sure we worm her and use flea control.*
- *Wash her if she gets smelly or dirty and dry her well.*
- *Never shout at her or make her feel anxious.*
- *Register her with the local authority.*
- *Make sure she is always wearing her collar or harness and identity disc.*
- *Arrange for her to be microchipped.*
- *Never let her out of the house and garden except when we can supervise her.*
- *Obey the local laws, especially with regards to where we can let Brook off the lead.*
- *Carry a poo bag when we go out and always pick up after her when she defecates.*
- **Be consistent with all of our dog rules so she doesn't get confused!**

Socialising your dog means giving it as many opportunities as possible to mix and play with other dogs – and people. This allows it to learn the social skills which are critical in today's society. The same principle applies to children.

Nowadays dog owners almost take the need to socialise their dogs for granted. But in 1981 when Ruth started training, it was a fairly new idea. Her late husband, David Weston, introduced the concept back in the 1970s after reading about the work of two psychologists in the USA, Professors Scott and Fuller. Scott and Fuller conducted a twenty-year study of dog behaviour which found that there was a critical time when dogs should be socialised: between three and twelve weeks of age. They called it the 'critical period' because a dog must be socialised during this time if it is to learn to relate with people and other animals as effectively as possible.

Since the publication of our first book, *Dog Training: The Gentle Modern Method* in 1990, the need for socialisation has become well recognised. In fact many veterinary surgery staff now run puppy pre-school at their clinics. This gives puppies a positive experience of going into the surgery and is an ideal opportunity for vet staff to educate people about the health needs of dogs, as well as provide some basic training.

The keys to socialising your dog

Start young

It gives you and your dog an enormous advantage if you acquire your puppy at seven or eight weeks of age and start to socialise it immediately. Some people worry their dog might get a contagious disease if they socialise it with

Chapter 10

Socialising
your dog

Dogs are more likely to be euthanased due to behavioural problems related to lack of socialisation than to die of infectious diseases.

other dogs before its immunisation regime is complete, but it is much harder for puppies to learn to cope with new experiences if they are kept isolated in the garden until fourteen weeks of age, when immunisation is complete. Consider the psychological health of your dog as much as its physical health. Many behavioural and temperament problems are a direct result of dogs not being socialised during the critical period. Timidity and aggression are typical problems in unsocialised dogs and can be extremely hard to cure.

Take your puppy everywhere you go when it is young and involve it in as many experiences as possible. This may include trips in the car and on buses and trains; visits to farms, cities and the beach; and exposure to people of all ages and a variety of different animals. These experiences will help your puppy encounter many of the sights, sounds and smells that it will come across during its life.

The ideal place to socialise your young dog is at a puppy school where young puppies can interact off the

Puppy school

lead in a safe environment. Puppy school gets your puppy accustomed to reading the body language of all different breeds and types of dogs, not just their own litter. This is critical, as dogs communicate with each other, and with us, mostly by reading body language. An ideal puppy school has pups of a similar age and size, and a large, safe, grassed outdoor area where they can interact without feeling penned in or becoming stressed.

Teach puppies not to bite

It is natural for puppies to bite and mouth each other (and humans), but they can be taught what is acceptable and what is not. If your puppy bites or mouths another puppy too hard, the other will tend to give a high-pitched squeal which says, 'Back off, you're biting too hard'. This feedback is an important part of your puppy acquiring good manners and teaching it bite inhibition. If you react in a similar way if a puppy puts its teeth on you, even gently, it will learn that you are fragile. Be careful never to reinforce a puppy for biting by giving it any sort of attention – good or bad. Give a squeal and *walk away*.

Puppy school helps to teach bite inhibition

Take away what the dog wants – that is, your company – and be absolutely consistent. Never allow your children to slap the dog if it mouths because this will only make it either more aggressive or more timid, depending on the dog's temperament.

Get puppies used to all types of people

It is important that your puppy is friendly with everyone. If your dog bites someone it will probably end up being put down, even if the person concerned was at fault; our society will always put the safety of people as their first priority. Early exposure to different people is critical: for example, your puppy could be exposed to elderly people, people in wheelchairs, people who wear hats and have beards, and people with special needs who may make erratic movements and who may not always be able to control their behaviour.

Even friendly dogs can be frightened by new experiences and bark in alarm. The most effective way to make people seem friendly to your puppy is to ask them to give it a small piece of food when it approaches them. Make sure the puppy is behaving in a desirable manner (for example, not jumping up) when they give it the food so they are reinforcing an appropriate behaviour. You might ask the person concerned to squat down to reinforce the dog so they are less threatening and there is less incentive for the puppy to jump up.

Get puppies used to other animals

Puppies should meet a whole range of animals, such as horses, chickens, cattle and cats, especially if they are likely to be exposed to them in later life. First, teach your dog to stay (see Lesson 6), then put it on the lead and

practise the stay with one animal, such as a horse, at a distance. Gradually reduce the distance between you and the horse. For more detail, see our previous books, *Dog Problems: The Gentle Modern Cure* and *Your Ideal Dog.*

Get your puppy used to other animals

Get puppies used to sights and sounds

Habituation is the process of getting your dog used to the sights and sounds it is likely to encounter in everyday life, such as the vacuum cleaner or lawnmower. Start by putting the vacuum cleaner on when your puppy is outside the house and gradually bring the puppy closer to the source of the sound. Reinforce the puppy for remaining quiet. Try putting the vacuum cleaner on when the pup is eating its dinner so it begins to associate the sound with the benefit of eating its meal. If your puppy looks afraid of the noise, respond by acting cheerfully and talking to the puppy in a confident manner so it gets the impression that there is nothing to be afraid of. If your puppy continues to appear afraid, you may have progressed too quickly and you may need to go back to a lower intensity of sound to build up the pup's confidence again.

Never allow your dog to chase any animals, even if you don't like the neighbour's cat! Chasing is self-rewarding, so once started, dogs will keep doing it.

Chapter 11

Health and hygiene

Having a dog as a pet has health and hygiene implications for your children. A number of these implications are actually positive, and the negative ones can be avoided by following a few simple rules.

Children who own pets have stronger immune systems than children who do not. A British study found that children with exposure to animals had more stable immune systems and were better at fighting off infections. These children also missed fewer days at school. This study supports what's known as the 'dirty hypothesis' which suggests that too much cleanliness during childhood can be detrimental to the immune system, causing it to be weaker later in life. It is suggested that this is one of the reasons for the soaring rates of childhood asthma.

The main hygiene risk associated with dog ownership is infections. Children generally have less resistance to infection than adults and can develop gastroenteritis more easily. They can pick up roundworm, hookworm or tapeworm from soil containing dog faeces, although in developed countries this is extremely rare. Worm infestation rarely causes severe symptoms but can cause discomfort and itching around the anus. This often results in scratching, contamination of the fingers and reinfection if children put their fingers in their mouths.

Take a few commonsense precautions to minimise the health risks:

◆ Don't let the dog lick your child's face.
◆ Encourage your children to wash their hands before eating.
◆ Don't allow the dog to lick the dishes.
◆ Don't allow your children to feed the dog from the dinner table. Train your dog to sit quietly when the family is eating and don't encourage it to beg for food.
◆ Don't allow young children to walk around with food in their hands. It is very difficult for a dog to resist taking food from a toddler's dangling hand!
◆ Avoid getting a puppy if you have a baby or toddlers – a puppy that isn't toilet-trained and children crawling around the floor are not a good combination.
◆ A healthy dog is less likely to pose a health problem to your children. Follow the simple guidelines below to keep your dog in top health.

The keys to maintaining your dog's health and hygiene

Immunise your dog

Generally speaking, puppies are immunised for the first time about two weeks before they go to their new home. Depending on the type of vaccine, the regime typically entails immunisation at six, twelve and sixteen weeks, followed by a booster each year. The immunisation regime will vary from country to country and even from one area of the country to another, so it is best to follow the advice of your local veterinarian.

Worm your dog

Once again, follow the advice of your vet who will have the necessary local knowledge. Often, a puppy is born with roundworm infection, and worming is carried out about every two weeks until the dog is about four months of age. Follow-up worming can vary depending on the dog's diet. (For example, farm dogs often eat rotting carcasses and may be more likely to get tapeworm infestation.)

Keep your dog and your environment free of fleas

Fleas can transfer easily from one dog to another, so use a product that has a residual effect in the skin. Fleas can cause allergic reactions in some dogs and this can set up a vicious scratch–itch cycle. If you are unfortunate enough to suffer a flea infestation, you will need to treat your dog's bed and other pets, and 'bomb' your house with an appropriate insecticide.

Grooming helps to keep your dog healthy

Groom your dog

Regular grooming stimulates your dog's skin and keeps it healthy. Frequent bathing (for instance, once a week) is unnecessary as it can remove the natural oils from the skin, although dogs do get smelly at times so a bath or shower may be in order. We recommend bathing your dog three to six times a year. When you bathe your dog, use a shampoo specifically designed for dogs as the pH balance of their skin is different from ours.

You can use a moisturising soap-free product if your dog tends to have itchy skin. Dry your dog well after its bath and keep it moving around to prevent it from getting cold.

Scabies or sarcoptic mange is a skin disease caused by mites which can be spread to humans. If your dog is itchy and looks moth-eaten, see your vet immediately.

Clip your dog's nails regularly unless they are worn down naturally.

Provide adequate exercise and play

It is ideal if your dog can be given free running (off-lead) exercise in a safe area away from traffic. If this is not possible, we suggest that you use a long lead or extension lead so that your dog can sniff and carry out some normal doggy behaviours.

Provide adequate exercise and play

Dispose of faeces

Try to condition your dog to defecate in one spot in the garden. Remove faeces from the garden as soon as possible – at least daily. Needless to say you should teach your children to pick up after the dog when you are out and remind them to wash their hands when they get home or carry disposable wipes. Some places provide poo bags and poo bins, but it's always best to carry a couple of plastic bags with you. Some local authorities fine you if you don't pick up your dog's poo.

Choose your dog carefully to avoid inherited health problems

Dogs can suffer from a number of genetically inherited diseases. If you are getting a puppy, check that its parents have been screened for the problems that are common in that particular breed of dog (see also Chapter 7).

Chapter 12

The death of a pet

Losing a loved pet is often a child's first experience of death. Some kids truly see their dog as a best friend and the grief associated with its death can be almost as devastating as if a human family member dies.

Parents can help children cope with the loss of a loved dog by explaining to them that all people and animals die, that it is a natural part of the life cycle and that it is okay to feel sad. It is important that children's feelings are acknowledged, as grief is a normal and natural response to death. It is an expression of love and a means of saying things like, 'I am sad that you are gone', and, 'I will miss you'. Children cope better with death when parents talk to them about it; children can sense if something is being hidden from them and this tends to make them worry more. Encourage your child to talk about their lost pet and their feelings about it for as long as they need to. Allow them to express all the emotions and feelings associated with grief: denial, anger, guilt, hostility, sadness and depression are all normal. And remember that all children react differently, so if a child does not cry or talk about the death that does not mean she is not mourning.

Let children ask the difficult questions like, 'Is our dog ever coming back?' or 'Did our dog die because I did something wrong?' Simple, truthful answers are best here. When it comes to death it is generally not helpful to tell your child something that she will have to 'unlearn' at a later date. Suggestions that 'death is like sleeping' or that 'God has chosen our dog to be an angel' are often not helpful, because children may develop concerns about going to sleep themselves or resent the God that has taken their pet away.

Parents also need to let their children cry. Crying is a normal response and suggesting, especially to male children, that they should be brave, will only force them to suppress the way they are feeling and slow the normal grief process. It is also okay to express your own emotions and to cry in front of your children. Showing your emotions will help your children express theirs.

Obviously you will explain death to your child in a way that is consistent with the religious and spiritual beliefs of your family. The detail of what you say is not critical, but it is important that your explanations are simple, comforting and consistent. Reassure your child that the dog had a happy life and is not experiencing any pain. Make sure she understands it is not her fault that the dog died. Answers to the question 'What does "dead" mean?' can include, 'She has stopped breathing and her body has stopped working. She can't feel or see or eat or play anymore'. Younger children in particular may not be able to take in the answers to their questions all at once. You may need to explain the same concepts over and over again. It is useful to keep repeating the same message in a consistent way and to use the same words for 'dead' and 'death' rather than using them interchangeably with terms like 'expired' or 'passed on'.

If a dog needs to be put down, explain to the children that it is okay to end the life of a dog if it is suffering, and that quality of life is more important than longevity.

All people cope better with loss if they have the

Children cope better with death when parents talk to them about it

opportunity to pay last respects and say goodbye. Remember to give this opportunity even to older, adult children who have left home, especially if they still retain some relationship with the dog. In some instances, saying goodbye may involve seeing the body or watching the dog being put down. In most cases, it can involve being a part of the burial ceremony. Many children like to write a poem about their pet, draw a picture, keep a lock of hair, plant a tree, frame a special photograph, share their thoughts with other family members, light a candle or gather a few of the pet's favourite toys for burial. All of these ceremonial activities aid the process of saying goodbye and help children to feel involved in celebrating the life of their pet and sharing their feelings of loss.

Children experience ups and downs when coping with loss. They might appear to be coping well, but then go through another period of feeling tearful and emotional. This can be sparked off by recalling a particular memory of their pet, seeing a dog that reminds them of their dog, or observing other children playing with their own pets. Do not tell your child that it is time he was over the dog or that he needs to move on. No time limits should be placed on grieving; children should be allowed to continue to express their feelings.

Some families are tempted to get a new pet immediately as it offers a distraction and can ease grief in the short term. We don't believe this is a good idea as it prevents the family from properly working through their loss. A number of people we know have also found that this can make it harder to bond with the new dog. Be guided by your child as to the best time to get a new pet. And don't treat it as a replacement for the lost animal but as a unique and special dog in its own right. Remember too that a young puppy will behave in a very different way to the mature older dog you probably had before!

Teaching kids how dogs learn

Depending on the age of your child, you may want to explain how dogs learn. This makes the training process more interesting and can help your child to produce and reward the behaviours you want and avoid creating behaviours you don't want. Children under the age of six can't really understand the method and it may be better simply to teach them to practise the 'come' and 'sit' with your trained dog.

Classical and operant conditioning are explained in Chapter 3. The following is how we explain the principles to primary school children:

We're going to teach your dog some different lessons so that it fits into the family and gets on with the neighbours. We do this by rewarding the dog when it does the right thing, such as coming to us when it's called. The proper term for this is 'reinforcement'. A reward or reinforcement is something the dog likes, and when it is associated with a particular behaviour, it makes that behaviour more likely to happen again in the future.

The
Lessons

Think what would happen if your teacher gave you a prize for writing a good story; you would be more likely to write a good story again to try to earn another reward. It makes you try hard to do well.

The way we reward a dog's behaviour is usually with food – at least to begin with. This is because dogs are more motivated by food than by any other reward. It is very important that your dog is hungry when you are teaching it new things, so it is very keen to earn the food rewards you are going to offer.

We use food in two very different ways when training.

Using food as an inducement

When we're teaching a new exercise, for example teaching the dog to come when it is called, we hold food between our fingers and drop our hand down low at the dog's eye level to get the dog to come to us. We call this food inducement. Food inducement is really just a way of getting the dog into the position that we want. If we didn't use food inducement we would have to wait until the dog came to us of its own accord, or we would have to force the dog to come to us. Using force isn't a good idea as neither dogs nor people respond well to being forced to do anything. On the other hand, if we do something voluntarily we will learn very quickly and willingly. We pair the food inducement with a hand and voice signal so that the dog comes to associate its behaviour (for example, coming) with a certain hand and voice signal and will learn to respond to the signals on their own in the future.

Using food as a reward or a reinforcement

When the dog does what you want, for example, comes to you, you reward or *reinforce* the dog with the food you have in your hand. The dog learns to associate the reward with

Never reward behaviours you don't want, for example, by feeding your dog when it begs at the table.

coming when it is called. So when you call the dog to you next time, it will remember the food reward it earned previously and will be more likely to repeat this behaviour.

Cutting out food inducement

Once your dog has practised a lesson a few times, it is really important to stop *using food in your hand* to *induce* the dog's response. This is because you don't want to get to the point where your dog will only get into the correct position when you have food in your hand. To achieve this, just use the hand and voice signal, then *reinforce* your dog with food after it does what you want.

Using intermittent rewards or reinforcement

When you get to the stage that your dog follows your hand and voice signals, you need to stop rewarding it with food *every time* it does what you want, and only reinforce it *sometimes*. This is called *intermittent reinforcement* and is a more effective way of training than rewarding every single response. It is a good idea to choose the 'best' responses to reinforce, for example, reward your dog if it comes to you quickly and as soon as you call it, rather than if it comes to you slowly after sniffing around a bit. This helps your dog understand exactly what it should do and the sorts of responses that you like the best.

Communicating with your dog

Dogs communicate and relate to people through their senses of sight, hearing, touch, taste and smell. But we have to keep in mind that the dog's senses are different from ours. Try to see things from the point of view of your dog and train it in a way that makes the best use of its senses.

The sense of sight

Think about the position of your dog's eyes compared with yours. They are set more to the side of their face, whereas yours are in the front. This means that you can focus very accurately, which is important if you want to read, use the computer or do your homework. In many ways your dog's vision is not as good as yours because the nose tends to get in the way when the dog is looking straight ahead. Put your fist in front of your nose and see what happens! However because the dog's eyes are set on the side of its face, it has a wider field of vision and is therefore very good at picking up movement.

It is very important to realise that dogs communicate with each other using body language. This means we need to use body language to communicate with them too. We do this in the form of hand signals.

What does this mean for training?

1   Make moving hand signals at your dog's *eye level*, because this makes them look more interesting. This is particularly important if you are practising a lesson such as calling your dog to come to you. If you stand still and do nothing, you will look pretty boring to your dog!

2   If your dog sees a jogger or cyclist or anything that is moving fast, it may be triggered to chase after them. You have to make yourself a lot more interesting to compete with that, perhaps by running away from your dog, then dropping your hand down low.

3   If your dog has a lot of hair hanging over its eyes, you may need to clip it or tie it back so it can see as well as possible.

4   Contrary to popular opinion, dogs aren't colour-blind. They can see violet, indigo and blue, but other colours look like shades of yellow. This means that your dog

may be able to see toys better if they contrast with the surroundings. For example, a blue ball will stand out from grass, which looks yellow to a dog.

The sense of hearing

The first thing you will notice about your dog's ears is that they are much bigger than yours. They are also mobile, so the dog can position them in such a way that they pick up sounds much more efficiently than you can. In fact, dogs can hear at least four times as well as humans. Dogs with erect ears can usually hear better than dogs with floppy ears. Dogs hear high-pitched noises better, because in the wild they had to hear the squeaks of prey animals.

Remember that dogs don't chat with one another so voice signals aren't as important to dogs as we like to think they are!

What does this mean for training?

1   Try to use soft voice signals, as your dog can hear very acutely and you don't want to use your voice as a threat.
2   Use a high-pitched tone so your dog can hear it better and to make your voice more exciting.
3   It's important that all family members use the same word when teaching their dog a lesson – otherwise it's like the dog having to learn more than one language.
4   Remember that your dog can hear things better than you, so it may be distracted by sounds that you don't even hear.
5   Dogs tend to react more to sounds which are important to them, such as the clanking of food bowls, the rattle of car keys and the fridge door opening. Sometimes you can use this to your advantage!

Dogs with pricked ears can usually hear better than dogs with floppy ears

There is a tendency in Western societies to feed dogs too much and too frequently, especially when they are puppies. As a result, many dogs grow unnaturally quickly and put on too much weight at an early age, which is detrimental to their health and longevity. Some become choosy about what they eat.

The following is a good guide to how often you should feed your dog.

- **8 to 10 weeks of age** *Maximum of three meals a day. (We never fed our dogs more than twice a day after they were eight weeks old, as this is more consistent with what would happen in a natural environment.)*
- **10 to 16 weeks of age** *Two meals a day.*
- **4 months onwards** *One meal a day (with the exception of very elderly dogs which may need to be fed frequently to maintain body weight).*

Feed your dog at a time that suits you and your family. Food should never be left in a dish so the dog can graze on it during the day. If a dog does not finish its meal in less than five minutes, it isn't hungry! A dog should eat like a wolf, that is, 'wolf it down'.

2 Prepare some small pieces of food that your dog really likes. Choose food that is not crumbly and doesn't need to be chewed. Dogs will learn to look down and snuffle the ground if you use crumbly food, as it is easily dropped, and if you use food that needs to be chewed, your dog may stop to eat it which interrupts the flow of your training. We find raw gravy beef to be excellent, but some people who are vegetarian are not comfortable with this, and may prefer to handle cold cooked sausage. Initially you can hold a few spare

When the kids do the training

It is very important that all family members use the same hand and voice signals so the dog does not get confused.

If your child is under eight years of age, we suggest you train the dog first and then teach your child how to do it. Remember that the best lessons for three- to six-year-olds to practise are come when called and sit. Many children of eight or older can train the dog themselves, particularly if an experienced handler helps them when they're starting off.

The most critical lessons to ensure safety and control are come when called, stay and heel (Lessons 1, 6, 7 and 8).

pieces of food in the hand you are not using to give hand signals, so you can reinforce your dog rapidly. Later on it is better to keep the food in a bumbag or your pocket (as long as you can get it out quickly).

3 Select a training area that is safe and free from traffic. A confined area such as a driveway or a narrow strip of garden is good to start with, as it helps you to shape the behaviour you want. A restricted environment helps your dog to concentrate on its lessons and prevents it from moving too far away from you. Soon you will be able to go further afield and feel confident that your dog will respond to you.

4 Train without distractions such as the presence of very young children and other dogs, at least initially.

5 Teach the first four lessons in the order shown, as they are prerequisites for some of the more complex lessons and we explain the training procedure in these chapters in more detail.

6 When you have taught your dog some lessons, try to practise them during your daily routine so the dog learns to respond to you in different situations, such as the house, garden, park and walking down the street. Don't feel you have to practise every day – do whatever suits your lifestyle. A two-minute training session, two to three times a week is quite sufficient.

Good luck…and remember, training should always be fun for all concerned!

Teaching the dog to come when it is called is probably the most important lesson for kids to practise. It is relatively simple to teach provided the dog is initially taught without distractions. We suggest that an adult or a child over eight teach the dog first by practising the lesson three or four times so it has learnt the exercise before showing a younger child how to do the same.

Teaching the lesson

Before you start, read the material at the beginning of this section about preparing the dog (and the kids!) for the training session.

Teaching your dog to come when called

The photographs show the dog handler giving a signal with their right hand because the majority of people are right-handed. However either hand can be used for most exercises.

1 Ensure that your dog is not too far away from you, and can see and hear you. Take a small piece of meat in your hand, making sure it is tucked well between your thumb and other fingers so it is not too obvious to the dog. Wait until your dog is looking at you.

2 Turn to face the dog and, if necessary, call its name in a high-pitched tone to gain its attention. As soon as the dog looks at you, drop the hand containing the food low to the ground in front of your legs. **Make sure you drop your hand early to give the dog a target to come towards.**

3 As the dog comes towards you, say 'come' **once only**.

4 When the dog reaches your hand, give it the piece of food immediately.

5 Return your hand to waist level.

6 Give the dog a 'free' signal by saying 'off you go' and fanning both hands out at your waist level above the dog's head.

Repeat steps 1 to 6 once or twice.

Practising the lesson

7   Stop using food in your hand as part of the signal, but hold a piece of food in your other (left) hand. Drop your **empty** hand low to the ground in front of your legs but otherwise keep your signal exactly the same as when you were using food.

8   Call 'come' as your dog moves towards you.

9   When the dog **first** comes to your empty hand, instantly reinforce it with food from your other hand. (This ensures that the dog earns the reward quickly when it correctly responds to the hand and voice signal without food inducement.)

10 Repeat steps 7 to 8 but reinforce your dog with food from your pocket or bumbag **intermittently**, choosing the quickest responses to reinforce.

Other considerations

◆   It is a good idea to offer a 'free' signal after your dog has returned to you to indicate to the dog that it has permission to move away. (Once you have taught more lessons, you can practise a variety of them at once so your dog learns to concentrate for longer, then offer your 'free' signals.)

◆   When you are out walking, avoid calling your dog to you **only** when it is time to go home, otherwise the dog may begin to associate coming with loss of freedom.

◆   Puppies up to twelve weeks of age are more likely to stay close to their owners for security. Mother Nature tells them that they are not strong enough to be out alone. Capitalise on this if you are training a young puppy.

◆   It is a good idea to change direction frequently when walking a young puppy. Don't make the puppy aware that you have changed direction by calling it, make it notice on its own. This will establish a very good habit for the future: you want your dog to be worrying where you are rather than vice versa. You can even go and hide behind a tree and let the puppy find you. Make a big fuss of the pup and reinforce it with food occasionally when it seeks you out.

- An older dog can be encouraged to come to you if you run off in the opposite direction so that it is triggered to chase after you. Don't run after your dog as it will probably regard this as a game and go faster and faster in the opposite direction!

- Never let your child fall into the trap of getting annoyed or punishing your dog if it doesn't return to her immediately. Explain that you realise It is frustrating but it will only make the dog less likely to want to come back to her in future. You may need to point out that your child doesn't always do what she is told either!

Possible problems	Possible causes	Suggested remedies
The dog runs off instead of coming. (See also 'The recalcitrant canine' on the next page)	The dog is not keen enough for food.	Read the section on pages 97–9 about preparing for training.
	Your hand and voice signals are not demonstrative enough.	Modify your signals to make them more obvious and exciting.
	Distracting stimuli.	Practise in an area well known to the dog and free of distractions.

Possible problems	Possible causes	Suggested remedies
The dog is fearful and reluctant to come.	Prior negative experience. Genetic factors.	Make sure your dog is particularly motivated for food. Walk away with your back to the dog holding food in your hand at your side. Feed the dog when it approaches, then move away. Repeat this numerous times. Then ask patient, dog-orientated friends to practise the same technique with your dog.
The dog comes rapidly, is reinforced, then moves off quickly.	The dog is not yet well conditioned.	Offer a 'free' signal before you allow the dog to move off. Gradually increase the time before you give this signal.
	The dog is not motivated by food or lacks concentration.	Make the dog extra keen for food next time.
	Distracting stimuli.	Practise without distractions initially and then gradually introduce them.

The recalcitrant canine

We can hear a few people saying, 'Yes, that's all very well, but what happens if my dog has really got into the habit of running off?' Needless to say it is extremely important to modify this behaviour, so your dog doesn't get involved in, or cause, an accident, and so you don't feel obliged to confine it to the backyard or a lead.

Our solution to this problem is based on changing the way you feed your dog for a while, so it doesn't get fed from its dish, but only when it responds to your call. This provides a great incentive for it to change its behaviour. You may find it helpful to practise the suggestions below with another dog who never runs off to start with.

Make sure your dog is very motivated for food by delaying its meal for a few hours. Put the dog's meal into six to ten different bags – it's important to reward your dog generously for this lesson, so don't be stingy with the food. Go out into an *enclosed area* to practise. Follow points 7 to 9 in Lesson 1, but give the dog *one bag of food* each time it responds to you. Then give the dog a 'free' signal. Repeat this with the other bags of food, gradually increasing the time before you give the 'free' signal, and finish for the day. The dog gets *nothing from its dish*. It *only* gets fed when it comes to you – and quickly!

Do a similar thing every time you feed the dog over the next few days, except reinforce the response intermittently. Be consistent – do not relent! Your dog will soon be thinking, 'If I come to you, it's great, if I don't there's nothing in it for me. I want to get to you as quickly as I can!'

Next you might take the dog into the garden and go through a similar procedure. Then progress to practising in a park that is safe from traffic. If you feel anxious about letting your dog go free, leave a long lead or piece of rope dangling from its collar until you gain confidence in its response.

Your dog should learn rapidly not to run off. Then you can go back to feeding it once a day from the dish. *However, you should still reinforce your dog intermittently for coming to you in different situations.*

If you have more than one dog, you will have to recondition them *individually*. It's important to remember that this regime may save your dog's life one day and won't do your dog any harm whatsoever. It still gets the same amount of food but only for responding to your 'come' signals.

Remember – intermittent reinforcement will keep your dog responding.

Children often inadvertently encourage dogs to jump by throwing their hands up in front of their face and giving them a target to jump towards. If your dog learns to sit in front of you, this won't be such a problem, as it can't both sit and jump at the same time. Once you have taught the lesson, practise it frequently when your dog is likely to jump, for example, when you come home and the dog is excited. Try to anticipate when it might jump and produce the sit before this occurs. You will need to carry some food with you so you can have it ready to reinforce the dog when it sits to greet you. This does take a bit of planning and co-ordination but the rewards are worth it.

Teaching your dog to sit in front of you

Teaching the lesson

1   Take a small piece of food in the hand you will use to give the signal. Drop this hand down in front of your legs to a point level with the dog's eyes. If necessary call 'come' or your dog's name to attract its attention.

2   When the dog reaches your hand, raise it immediately to chest level by sliding it up close to your body so that your dog looks up and consequently starts to sit. Bring your body upright at the same time.

3   Say 'sit' **once only** as your dog starts to sit.

4   Reinforce your dog with the food you are holding in your hand the moment its bottom touches the ground.

5   Return your hand to waist level.

Repeat steps 1 to 5 once or twice.

Practising the lesson

6   Stop using food in your hand as part of the signal, but hold a piece of food in your other hand. Drop your empty hand down in front of your legs to a point level with the dog's nose. Make sure you

Teaching your dog to sit in front of you is the best cure for jumping up.

don't change the look of your hand signal because you aren't holding food.

7   Raise your hand up to chest level and say 'sit'.

8   Reinforce the dog **immediately** with the piece of food from your other hand the **first** time it responds to the voice and hand signal.

9   Repeat steps 6 to 8 but reinforce the dog **intermittently** with food from your pocket or a bumbag, choosing quick, straight sits to reinforce.

Remember to offer the 'free' signal if you are giving the dog permission to move away.

It is very important that you don't get the dog to sit by pushing its bottom down. The dog must sit *voluntarily* in order to draw a connection between the sit and the reinforcement you give it.

Some dogs sit more readily because of their anatomical structure. Some breeds with long legs may be harder to condition. Dogs such as greyhounds, for example, don't naturally sit very often. Try holding your hand above your dog's head for ten to fifteen seconds. This will make your dog look up for longer and it should start to sit. Offer a generous reward when it does.

Possible problems	Possible causes	Suggested remedies
The dog jumps at your hands.	You are leaving your hand dangling above the dog's nose.	Make a clean, flowing signal up to chest level. Reinforce with a quick, precise movement then take your hand back to waist level.
The dog does not seem to follow the hand signal.	Your hand signal may be too rapid.	Give a slower signal.
	Eyesight not fully developed in a young pup.	Delay training until after eight weeks of age.
	The dog has poor vision or is blind.	Get a veterinary check-up.

Possible problems	Possible causes	Suggested remedies
The dog sits crookedly.	Your hand signal may be too rapid.	Leave your hand down at the dog's eye level until it reaches you and stops. (If necessary, take one or two steps back to straighten the dog up.) Then raise your hand up to chest level.
		Only reinforce straight sits.
	Your dog may be running towards you too quickly.	Call your dog when it's only a few paces away at first, so it does not build up too much speed as it comes towards you.
	Your dog may be coming towards you at an angle.	Practise between two parallel benches to start with.
		Turn to face your dog before you drop your hand down to the dog's eye level. Then raise your hand to chest level.

Practise beside a low barrier if your dog sits crookedly

Teaching your dog to sit at your side

This lesson is important as a precursor to teaching the sit stay. It is also a useful base for the more complex lessons such as walking your dog beside you. We teach dogs to sit on the left side as most people tend to walk their dog on the left. The historical reason for this is that men who used dogs for hunting traditionally held their gun in their right hand, so the dog walked on the opposite side.

Teaching your dog to sit at your side is relatively easy once you have taught it to sit in front. From the dog's perspective the signals are very similar. It may help if you practise the hand signal while looking in a mirror before you start teaching your dog. Sometimes it's hard to train yourself and the dog at the same time!

Teach the lesson while standing still first of all, rather than while you are on the move. Once you have got it right, you can sit your dog at your side during walks, such as when you come to a road and are waiting for a car to pass.

Teaching the lesson

1   Take a small piece of food in your right hand.

2   Turn your back to your dog. Call it to your left side by placing your right hand across the front of your body at the dog's eye level and if necessary make a noise, such as a click with your tongue, to attract the dog to look at you. The dog will move to stand at your left side provided you make the hand signal obvious. You and your dog should be facing the same direction. It is important that your hand is **level** with your left knee, not in front of the knee.

3   Draw your right hand upwards **directly above the dog's head** to approximately chest level. Your dog will tend to look up and move into the sit position.

4   Say 'sit' as soon as the dog starts to sit.

5   Reinforce it immediately its bottom hits the ground with food from your hand.

6   Move your hand back to a position in front of your waist.

Repeat steps 1 to 5 two or three times.

Practising the lesson

7   Stop using food as an inducement, but keep your hand and voice signal the same.

8   Reinforce your dog with food from your bumbag or pocket the **first** time it responds to the hand and voice signal.

9   Then reinforce your dog intermittently, choosing the best responses to reinforce, such as when your dog sits quickly in the correct position on the **first** signal.

Possible problems	Possible causes	Suggested remedies
The dog sits crookedly.	Your hand signal is crooked.	Make sure your signal is given directly above the dog's head and not slightly in front of you; 5–10 centimetres (2–4 inches) can make all the difference. Check it in a mirror!
	The dog runs into position too fast so your hand ends up in front of your left knee rather than level with it.	Take a step forward to get the dog level with your left knee before raising your hand directly above the dog's head (step 3).
	Your dog already has the habit of sitting crookedly.	Practise beside a low barrier such as a bench or table set on its side, so the dog sits parallel to both you and the bench.

Never reinforce your dog for sitting on an angle. |

Lesson 4

Teaching your dog to stand is probably less important than many other lessons, but it is useful to be able to stop your dog in the stand position during heeling or to take a photograph.

Teaching the lesson

1   Start with the dog sitting at your left side (see Lesson 3).

2   Take a small piece of food in your right hand.

3   Swing your hand forward about half a metre (20 inches) in front of your dog's nose as you take a small step forward with your left leg. Make a hand signal with your right hand which acts like a blocker in front of your dog's face with all your fingers extended. (The reward can be held against your palm with your thumb.)

4   Say 'stand' as soon as your dog begins to stand and leave your hand in front of your dog for two to three seconds so it doesn't move forward.

Teaching your dog to stand

5   Immediately reinforce the dog when it stands, with
    the food from your right hand. Remove your hand
    by swinging it across the front of your body **at the
    dog's nose level** before returning it to waist level.
    (If you remove your hand from in front of the dog's
    face directly to a position at waist height, you are,
    in effect, giving the dog a 'sit' signal.)

Repeat steps 1 to 5 two or three times.

Practising the exercise

6   Stop using food as an inducement. Offer the hand
    and voice signal only. Remember that your hand
    signal should **remain in front of the dog for two to
    three seconds** so your dog is stationary before you
    take your hand away.

7   Reinforce your dog intermittently, choosing the best
    responses (remaining standing in the correct
    position) to reinforce. Remember to give the 'free'
    signal whenever you give your dog permission to
    move away.

Possible problems	Possible causes	Suggested remedies
The dog sits immediately after standing.	The dog is looking up at you.	Stand the dog on a slight incline so that it stretches its back legs out behind it to balance and is less likely to sit.
The dog anticipates the sit.	You have been practising a predictable sequence of exercises, for example, asking it to sit then stand, then sit then stand again.	Do a series of stands without any sits between them. Introduce the stand stay (see Lesson 6) after you have taught the sit stay or drop stay.
The dog moves forward instead of remaining in the stand position.	You have removed your hand too quickly from in front of your dog's face.	Try leaving your hand in front of the dog for longer and reinforce your dog with food from the other hand before it has a chance to move forward. OR Take four or five pieces of food in your right hand. Stand the dog and feed it *one* piece. Withdraw your hand briefly at the dog's nose level, then feed another piece and so on.
	The dog is hyperactive.	Practise *after* a walk when the dog is tired!
The dog stands in front of you instead of at your left side.	Your hand signal is in front of your legs.	Make sure your hand signal is given directly in *front* of the dog's face, *level with your left knee*, not slightly in front of your body.
	You are pulling your hand away with food in it.	Give your dog the piece of food as soon as it stands. Stop using a food inducement after two or three successful stands.

Teaching your dog to lie down

This is a fantastic exercise for children to practise as it helps the dog to learn that the child is the one in control. Being 'in control' should not be confused with being rough or gruff with the dog. We try to explain to children that their brains are more developed than the dog's brain, so to be in control all they have to do is practise a few simple lessons with the dog, reinforcing it for doing what the child has asked it to do.

Teaching the lesson

1   Sit your dog at your left side (see lesson 3). (It is much easier for a dog to lie down from the sit position than from a stand.)

2   Take a small piece of food in your **right** hand. (This is one exercise where it is difficult to get your left hand into the correct position, so even left-handed people should use their right hand when teaching this lesson.)

3   Quickly bring your right hand to a position in front of the dog's nose.

4   Take a short step forward with your left leg at the same time as you move your hand slowly and obliquely down towards the ground. Turn the palm of your hand down so the food is between your hand and the ground. Leave about 3 centimetres (1 inch) between the ground and the palm of your hand to allow your dog to get its nose under your hand. Bend your knees so that you can get into the correct position.

5   Say 'drop' the moment that your dog starts to
    buckle at the front legs.

6   Reinforce the dog as soon as it starts to lie down.

7   Take your hand away at **ground** level in front of the
    dog's paws until you can bring it up beside the
    right side of your body without the dog noticing it.

8   Repeat steps 1 to 7 a few times, gradually keeping
    your dog down longer before you reinforce it.

Practising the lesson

9   Cut out food inducement as usual, and reinforce
    quick, straight drops intermittently.

10 Start to practise the drop stay (see Lesson 6) as a
    means of reinforcing your dog for staying down for
    a period of time.

11 Once the dog has dropped a few times, modify your
    signal by lifting your hand slightly above the dog's
    nose then bringing your hand rapidly down to
    within about 3 centimetres (1 inch) of the ground.
    This tends to make the dog throw its legs out in
    front and drop quickly.

Other considerations

◆ It is not natural for a dog to eat anything except bones in the drop position which can make this lesson a little more difficult to teach.

◆ The anatomy of some dogs can make it harder for you to induce them to lie down, for example, dogs with long gangly legs may take a little longer to condition. Sometimes it is necessary to reinforce successive approximations to the drop using shaping techniques (see Chapter 3). This means you might start by rewarding the dog for simply flexing its head downwards and gradually extend your expectations as your dog comes closer to achieving a proper drop.

Possible problems	Possible causes	Suggested remedies
The dog stands up instead of lying down.	You are moving your hand too rapidly towards the ground or too far in front of the dog.	Take your hand signal down on an imaginary line from in front of the dog's nose to a point just in front of where the dog's paws will be when it is lying down. It's a question of trial and error to some extent.
The dog's bottom rises up in the air as the nose and front legs go down.	Your hand signal goes right down to the ground.	Flatten your hand out about 3 centimetres (1 inch) *above* the ground so that your dog can get its nose underneath. This will usually make it collapse into the drop position.

Possible problems	Possible causes	Suggested remedies
The dog grabs food out of your hand before it reaches the drop position.	Using fresh meat, as it can be slippery for you to hold onto.	Try using a large piece of dry food instead of fresh meat *just until your dog is conditioned.*
The dog doesn't drop, in spite of your best efforts.	The dog may not be sufficiently motivated to earn the food rewards.	Delay the dog's mealtime and practise just before it is due.
	The anatomy of the dog may make it more difficult, for example, long gangly limbs.	Reinforce successive approximations to the drop delaying the reinforcement until the dog is further down each time. Sit on the floor with your legs bent up creating a tunnel. Induce the dog into the tunnel with food in your hand and reinforce it when it drops down. You can do a similar thing under a table.
	Small dogs can be hyperactive and move out of the sit position before you have a chance to practise the drop.	Place your dog on a table so it cannot move too far away. (Make sure the table's surface isn't slippery.) Drop your right hand down below the level of the tabletop. Most dogs will lie down quickly to get to the food.

Lesson **6**

The stay is one of the three exercises that we consider is critical to teach your dog. It reinforces passive behaviour and teaches the dog that you are the one in control of the situation, but in a very friendly way. It also teaches your child that if he is quiet the dog will be too – it's a lovely lesson for them to practise together. It is usually very easy once the dog is conditioned, provided that the child is consistent and does not have unrealistic expectations about how long he can expect the dog to stay or how far he can move away from the dog.

Teaching the lesson

The sit stay

1   Eliminate any distractions such as small children and other pets when you first practise this, as it is particularly important that your dog doesn't move in this exercise.

2   Sit your dog at your left side. Have your hands at waist level in front of you and have a few pieces of food ready in your right hand to offer as a quick reinforcement.

Teaching your dog to stay still

3　Say 'stay' then simply reinforce the dog for not moving. Don't move yourself at all. (Don't introduce a hand signal at this stage as it may encourage the dog to move. Don't use food inducement for this lesson as you don't want your dog to do anything except remain still.)

4　Say 'stay', then step forward half a pace with your **right** leg, keeping your left leg still. Before the dog attempts to move, step back to your original position beside the dog and reinforce it immediately. (Your right leg becomes a signal to the dog that means 'don't move' as it is the one further away from the dog.)

5　Repeat steps 2 to 4 a few times, gradually increasing the distance you move away from the dog to one, two, three paces and so on.

6　When you can get about four paces away, turn and face your dog, then return to your **original** position and reinforce it.

Practising the lesson

The sit stay

7　Practise going away from the dog in different directions and out of sight.

8 Introduce intermittent reinforcement in the same way as for the previous lessons.

9 Introduce the hand signal only when your dog has thoroughly learnt the lesson. Put your hand in front of the dog's face like a blocker as you say 'stay'. Make sure you return your hand to waist level **before** you move off.

The drop stay

The drop stay is taught and practised in the same way as the sit stay. Signal your dog to lie down then repeat steps 3 to 9 as above.

The stand stay

The stand stay is also taught and practiced in the same way as the sit stay – signal your dog to stand then repeat steps 3 to 9. You can make it easier for yourself if you try the following:

Stand the dog with its front feet on a step or mat so its front feet are higher than its rear. The back legs will extend to maintain the dog's centre of gravity, which makes it less likely to sit or move forward.

Stand your dog on an incline to prevent it from sitting or moving forward

Other considerations

◆ Use the word 'stay' **only** when you actually mean that your dog should remain in the same place and the same position until you return, otherwise the dog may become confused. Teach your child not to tell the dog to 'stay' as they leave for school, for example!

◆ Be extremely observant and note any body language which may herald movement from the stay position, such as head or ear movement or a wagging tail. Return to your dog quickly if you feel that it might move.

- Practise in different environments once the dog is conditioned, and introduce distractions such as other people, children, other dogs and food.
- If necessary, practise the stay when your dog is tired and unlikely to want to move.
- If your dog does move, make sure your child doesn't blame the dog. Simply tell him to go back to the beginning and re-teach the exercise.
- Make sure you ask your child to keep his voice signal quiet, as dogs have excellent hearing. Children sometimes raise the volume of their voice in the mistaken belief that it will make the dog understand better. I try to explain this by saying, 'Raising your voice will only stress the dog and make it less able to learn quickly. If you were learning a foreign language you would get stressed if the teacher shouted at you when you didn't understand'.

Possible problems	Possible causes	Suggested remedies
The dog moves forward as you move away.	The dog is very active.	Repeat step 3 a number of times and then build up the exercise gradually.
		Try practising in the drop stay, because dogs are usually more settled when lying down.
	You are moving your hands without realising it.	Keep your hands still at waist level except when you are reinforcing.
	You are moving your legs too far away too quickly.	Only take a few steps away from your dog to start with.

Possible problems	Possible causes	Suggested remedies
The dog moves forward as you return.	You are reinforcing the dog when you are in front of it.	Always return to a position *beside* the dog before reinforcing it.
The dog jumps up from the *drop* stay position.	You are lifting your hand up above the dog's head as you stand upright.	After you have reinforced the dog make sure you take your hand away at *ground* level, then stand upright. Try encouraging the dog to stay by placing a piece of food between its paws before you move off. Only do this a few times to re-teach your dog.
	You are working on an uncomfortable or wet surface.	Some dogs hate to drop on wet ground. Practise in a drier area.
The dog moves away while in the *stand* stay position.	The stand is not thoroughly conditioned.	Practise an extended stand. Leave your hand in front of the dog for longer and reinforce it with food from the other hand before it has a chance to move away. Place the dog's front legs higher than its back legs during the initial training (see the stand stay). Try placing a small bar of wood on the ground in front of the dog's front paws so it is less likely to move forward. This will give you more time to reinforce the desired behaviour.

It is particularly important that a dog doesn't pull on the lead if it is going to be exercised by children. (Although even if your dog walks calmly on the lead, you should always supervise primary school children when they take the dog out.) This lesson requires good timing and co-ordination. When we are helping to teach dog handlers this exercise we invariably ask them to simulate the movements with us without the dog a few times. This helps them to practise the correct actions. Teaching your dog and learning the lesson yourself at the same time can be quite a challenge!

Teaching the lesson

It is better to teach the dog to walk beside you off the lead to begin with, as leads can trigger dogs to pull. Practise in a confined area free from traffic at first.

1   Start with your dog at your left side. Keep your hands at waist level, except when you are giving a hand signal or offering reinforcement. Carry a few

Teaching your dog to heel off the lead

pieces of food in the hand that is not giving signals. (You will usually find it is not necessary to use food inducement for this lesson, because your dog will naturally tend to follow you when you walk off anyway.)

2　Step off with your left leg in a fairly bold, natural manner as if you were going for a walk, to encourage your dog to follow your movement. (You can swing your right or left hand forward in front of your dog's face at eye level at the same time as you step off if you wish, but this may cause some active dogs to jump up towards the hand.)

3　Say 'heel' the moment the dog takes up a position beside your left knee, so the word is paired with the correct position. Transfer a small piece of food into your right hand as you walk.

4　Take two or three more steps with the dog in the heel position, then stop in the stand position and reinforce your dog immediately its head is level with your **left knee**. Return your hand to waist level.

(At this stage don't worry about offering a verbal 'stand' signal, simply reinforce the dog for heeling in the correct position.)

5   Repeat steps 1 to 4 five or six times.

Practising the lesson

6   Gradually alter the distance the dog has to walk before it is offered reinforcement.

7   When the dog is heeling well, start offering a 'sit' or 'stand' signal when you stop, and reinforce the response intermittently with food from your pocket or bumbag. However you should sometimes go back to reinforcing your dog just for walking beside you, as you did when you were teaching the lesson.

Other considerations

◆   Practise in different environments so your dog gets used to walking beside you in different places. Don't practise for too long or the dog may get bored. Give your dog the 'free' signal, then introduce a game or different activity, then have another short heeling practice session if you want to.

◆   Your dog doesn't need to start heeling from a static position only. If it is running towards you, you can call it to your left-hand side and move off quickly together. In this way you are often able to reinforce a really enthusiastic response.

◆   When you are out for a walk and your dog spontaneously walks beside your left leg, reinforce it instantly. It is always a great idea to capitalise on desirable behaviours rather than paying attention to the dog only when it does something you don't want.

Possible problems	Possible causes	Suggested remedies
The dog moves away from your left side.	Distracting stimuli.	Minimise distractions by working in a familiar and restricted environment when you first teach the lesson.
	You are taking too many steps before reinforcing.	Practise heeling for short distances to start with and time your reinforcement to coincide with the dog being in the correct position.
	You are practising for long periods of time.	Always keep training sessions short and sweet! Make training fun, not hard work.
The dog lags during heeling.	You are stopping each time your dog lags.	Keep moving to encourage your dog to follow you. Reinforce it as soon as it has walked two to three paces in the correct position. Gradually increase the distance before you reinforce.
	You are moving too rapidly, especially when moving off.	Take steps which are relative to the dog's size, that is, small steps for a small dog.
	You have reinforced the dog for lagging in the past.	Sweep your right hand forward at the dog's eye level as you set off to stimulate your dog more. Reinforce it after two to three paces, before it has a chance to lag.

Possible problems	Possible causes	Suggested remedies
The dog surges forward during heeling.	Your hand signal is too demonstrative.	Do not use a hand signal. Reinforce with your left hand *before* your dog surges. (You can get your left hand into position more quickly than your right.)
	Some breeds, such as border collies, naturally seem to walk ahead of the handler.	When the dog gets ahead of you, turn right 180 degrees and move off in the opposite direction. You are now ahead of the dog. Reinforce the dog when it comes to a position next to your left leg, *before* it surges.
	The dog is more interested in its surroundings than in training.	Make sure the dog has plenty of opportunities to play and investigate off the lead so it is calmer during training.
The dog walks wide during heeling.	Some of the herding dogs have a tendency to do this due to their genetic programming.	Start training at eight weeks of age if you can so you can shape the behaviour you want. If the dog's behaviour is established, try practising in a narrow corridor so you use the environment to help to shape the behaviour you want. Outside, you can walk beside a low wall or beside the gutter of a pavement to give you a similar advantage.

Lesson 8

Teaching your dog to heel on the lead

When your dog has learnt to walk beside you off the lead, clip the lead onto its collar and simply practise steps 1 to 7 of the heeling off-lead exercise. Try to keep a nice loop in the lead between you and the dog. Avoid using the lead as a training aid by pulling the dog forward or back with it. You will be less inclined to do this if you loop the lead over the arm that you are not using to reinforce your dog, or if you put the end of the lead in your pocket or through your belt.

Some dogs can get very excited when they antici-pate going for a walk, which can make it hard to clip the lead on. If you have this problem, practise the following as a separate lesson a few times. It is easier to teach with the help of another person.

Clipping the Lead On

Teaching the lesson

1 Sit the dog in front of you.

2 Ask another person to quietly approach the dog, holding the lead. As your friend approaches, say 'wait' and feed your dog for remaining in the sit position *at the same time* as your friend clips on the lead.

3 Repeat steps 1 and 2 two or three times.

Follow the same procedure for removing the lead.

Practising the lesson

4 Stop using food as an inducement. Say 'wait' as your friend clips on the lead, then reinforce the dog for remaining still, *after* the lead has been clipped on.

5 You should now be able to take over the role of putting the lead on yourself, but don't forget to reinforce good responses *intermittently*. Remember if we don't reinforce behaviours occasionally, they will be much less reliable.

Heeling while pushing a pram or stroller

Make sure your dog walks well on a loose lead before you try this. It's a good idea to practise walking your dog beside a pram or stroller without a child in it to begin with. Practise in a quiet area free from traffic.

1 Put your dog on the lead and loop the lead over your left wrist.

2 Step off with your left leg, saying 'heel' as you push the pram forward.

3 Take a few steps, then reinforce your dog when it is in stand position beside your left leg. Stop while you do this to give your dog time to eat the food.

Never tie your dog up to a pram or stroller, however reliable the dog appears to be. It might be the one time your dog gets distracted and runs off, taking the pram with it!

4　When your dog is heeling well beside the pram, start offering a 'sit' or 'stand' signal when you stop, and reinforce the response intermittently with food from your pocket or bumbag.

When you feel confident with walking your dog and an empty pram or stroller, you will be ready to take your child out in it.

The recalcitrant canine

Some dogs have learnt to pull like a train when on the lead! If this describes your dog, practise heeling in a restricted area to begin with and ensure your dog is very motivated for the food rewards you are going to offer – that is, hungry!

If you have longstanding problems with heeling it may be helpful to engage a professional dog trainer to show you how to reshape your dog's behaviour. Choose a trainer who trains exclusively using positive reinforcement methods. Never use electronic or other aversive devices such as head collars or choker chains which put pressure on the dog's nose or neck to teach it to heel on the lead. We don't believe parents should be teaching kids to use punishment devices for the reasons discussed in Chapter 3.

Children can become overly excited when they are running and jumping with their dog so you may want to be a bit selective about whether you want to teach them how to do this lesson.

Teaching the lesson

1   Sit the dog at your left side in front of a *low* jump, no more than 15–20 centimeters (5–8 inches) high. Make sure the dog is right in the *middle* of the jump.

2   Take a piece of food in your hand. Thrust your hand forward and throw the food over the centre of the jump so the dog can see it clearly.

3   Say 'over' as the dog jumps.

4   The dog will be instantly reinforced when it jumps and reaches the food.

5   Practise steps 1 to 4 with a variety of low obstacles.

Practising the lesson

6   Phase out throwing food for your dog, but continue to use a similar hand signal and the word 'over'. Reinforce the dog with food from your pocket or bumbag intermittently after it has jumped. You will need to move forward as your dog jumps so you can reinforce it. Most dogs love this lesson, so food rewards are not often necessary. (Jumping seems to be intrinsically reinforcing.)

7   If you want, you can then set up an obstacle course.

Teaching your dog to jump

Walk towards the first obstacle with your dog in the heel position so that it is approaching the centre of the jump. When you are two or three paces away offer the usual hand and voice signal. Quickly move around the edge of the jump as your dog jumps over it. Reinforce your dog. Then approach the other jumps in the same manner and start to reinforce your dog intermittently.

Other considerations

Make sure your child doesn't ask the dog to jump something that is too high or could injure the dog in any way. As a rough guide, dogs without physical problems can usually jump to the height of their shoulder. Dogs with hip or elbow dysplasia should not be encouraged to jump.

Possible problems	Possible Causes	Suggested Remedies
The dog runs around the jump and is reinforced for not jumping.	The jump may be too high.	Lower the jump.
	It is not a natural behaviour for dogs to jump in the wild. They would normally choose to go round an obstacle as it is safer.	Jump the jump with your dog once or twice. Make it fun!
		If necessary set up some wing-type barriers at both sides of the jump.
The dog doesn't seem motivated to jump.	The food was not easily seen when thrown.	Try using a fairly large piece of food.
	The dog may have a physical problem which makes it painful for it to jump.	Get a veterinary check-up.

This is a fun exercise for your child to practise with your dog. Most dogs love this lesson because you reward their retrieving by throwing the article again so the game continues. Practise with something sausage-shaped which protrudes from the dog's mouth a bit so you can grab it easily without having to put your hand in amongst the teeth. One instructor we know makes up a simple toy out of a piece of stick with sheepskin sewn around it. One end of the stick can be covered with tape so the dog is less likely to pick it up at that end, making it easy for the person to grab it. The dogs love it!

Teaching the lesson

1   Choose a toy for your dog to retrieve which it likes to pick up in its mouth and which has the characteristics suggested above.

2   Get the dog excited about the toy by moving it around on the ground in front of it.

Teaching your dog to fetch and give

3   Throw the toy a short distance, making sure the dog clearly sees it being thrown.

4   Allow the dog to chase after the toy.

5   As the dog runs towards the toy, move forward so you are a few paces behind it when it picks the toy up. Make sure you do not distract your dog by being too close.

6   When the dog picks up the toy, pair this action with the word 'fetch' *then* turn and move away with short rapid steps. This will trigger the dog to chase after you.

7   Allow your dog to gain on you but *keep your hands up at waist level*. As the dog reaches you, turn and drop your hand down low and take the toy *directly* from the dog's mouth, saying 'give' as your dog releases it. (If necessary, offer a piece of food to entice your dog to drop the toy into your hand.)

8   Reinforce your dog either by doing another retrieve or giving it a piece of food.

9   Repeat steps 1 to 8 a few times, but end the game before your dog (or child) gets tired of it.

Other considerations

◆   Be particularly careful if you use food to teach your dog to give up the toy or to reinforce it. If you drop your hands too early, the dog may learn to drop the toy at a distance away from you. Try to time the exercise so you teach the dog to give the toy directly into your hand right from the start.

◆   Retrieving is reinforcing for most dogs but you may want to offer a 'bonus reinforcement' from time to time, especially for the last retrieve of the day. 'Bonus reinforcement' means giving your dog one piece of food, then another, then another – as many as you want.

◆   Retrieving is a great way of exercising your dog without you having to do too much. You can use a tennis racquet or a ball thrower for a longer retrieve.

◆   For best results introduce retrieving when the dog is very young.

◆   Make sure your child never scolds the dog for picking up something it is not allowed to have as this may make your dog reluctant to retrieve. Teach her to take preventative action instead by removing things before the dog sees them, and explain that you had to do the same thing when *she* was young.

Possible problems	Possible causes	Suggested remedies
The dog doesn't want to pick things up.	The dog isn't a natural retriever. The dog didn't learn the lesson when it was young. The dog has a history of being punished for picking things up.	Try tying a piece of string onto the end of your toy, then pull it along the ground. This will often set up a hunt–chase response. Make it as much fun as you can. Once your dog is picking the toy up, you can start practicing steps 1 to 9.
	If you have two dogs, one of them may always 'win' the toy and the other learns to give up.	Practise with the 'losing' dog by itself.
The dog runs off with the toy.	Children chasing the dog when it has the toy in its mouth.	Ask your children not to chase the dog, as this reinforces a behaviour you do not want. Teach the dog to give as a separate exercise. Sit the dog in front of you and offer the toy with one hand but *don't let go of it*. When the dog grabs the other end of the toy, offer food with your other hand and say 'give' as the dog relinquishes the toy. Repeat this a few times. (Make sure the toy is wide enough that the dog doesn't grab your hand instead of the toy!) Then practice steps 1 to 9 in a corridor, by throwing the toy up to the closed end. The dog has nowhere to go but back to you.

This is another fun exercise which can be useful when grooming the dog or checking its belly. It also reinforces the dog for going into a subordinate position, so it is a particularly appropriate exercise for your child to practise with the dog.

Teaching the lesson

1 Drop the dog (see Lesson 5).

2 Bend down in front of the dog. Have a piece of food in your right hand.

3 Place your right hand to the side of the dog's face so it is motivated to turn its head towards your hand. Reinforce the dog for twisting its head around towards its back.

4 Gradually bring your hand further around towards the back of the dog's neck, reinforcing the dog for getting further round each time.

Teaching your dog to roll over

5 You can stop at the point where the dog is lying on its back or take your hand even further over so that it rolls over completely. As your dog rolls, say 'roll over' and reinforce the dog with food when it has finished the roll.

6 Repeat steps 1 to 5 a few times, then stop using a food inducement and reinforce quick roll-overs intermittently in response to your hand and voice signal. Speed up the hand signal until it looks as if you are drawing a circle in the air in front of the dog.

Possible problems	Possible causes	Suggested remedies
The dog stands up when it twists its head towards its back.	You are lifting your hand too high as you try to get the dog to twist its head towards its back.	Squat down low as you teach the exercise. Keep your hand signal low as you bring it behind the dog's neck.
The dog seems reluctant to twist its head.	The dog has a physical problem such as arthritis.	The dog cannot learn this lesson.

This is mostly a fun lesson with few practical applications. Children love to show their friends this little trick, and if their friends also practise the exercise, your dog will welcome them coming to visit you.

'Shake'

Teaching the lesson

1   Sit your dog in front of you.

2   Place a piece of food in your clenched hand in front of the dog and about 5 centimetres (2 inches) above the floor. This will generally make the dog lift its foot to paw at your hand.

3   As the dog lifts its paw, say 'shake' and instantly turn your hand over and open your fist to release the food.

4   Repeat steps 1 to 3 two or three times, gradually making your hand signal higher depending on the height of your dog. Most dogs can comfortably lift their paw to the height of their shoulder.

Teaching your dog to shake hands and do 'High 5'

Practising the lesson

5 Stop using food as an inducement and change your hand signal to an open palm rather than a closed fist. Say 'shake' and gently shake the dog's paw. Reinforce your dog intermittently for responding to the hand and voice signal.

'High 5'

◆ Train the dog to shake then gradually lift your hand signal higher and make it more like a stop sign. Reinforce the dog intermittently for touching your hand with its paw.

Possible problems	Possible causes	Suggested remedies
The dog does not paw at your hand, so you cannot reinforce the response.	The dog is not motivated by food.	Try the exercise when the dog is hungry.
	The dog has been punished for pawing.	Lift the dog's paw gently and reinforce it with food at the same time. Repeat this a few times. Then wait until the dog lifts its paw spontaneously and instantly reinforce it.

It is useful for children aged six and above to feed the dog regularly because the dog will then associate them with food and consequently regard them as pretty important members of the family. If your child is six or seven, train the dog first and then your child can take over the task once the lesson is well learnt. Monitor this activity closely so that your child never gives the dog its meal when it is exhibiting an undesirable behaviour, such as barking. The ideal time to start this type of training is when the dog is very young, preferably between eight and twelve weeks of age.

Lesson

13

Teaching the lesson

1   Get an *empty* food bowl ready.

2   Sit the dog at your left-hand side. Take a small piece of the dog's favourite food in your *left* hand.

3   Feed the dog with the delicious morsel from your left hand as you place the empty bowl on the floor in front of it with your right hand. Say 'leave it' then quickly pick up the bowl before your dog shows too much interest in it. If your dog is extremely food-orientated you may have to start by putting the bowl halfway down to the floor and get it down to floor level gradually (shaping).

4   Repeat step 3 a few times.

5   Next, get to the stage where you can put the bowl down on the floor as you say 'leave it' and *then* reinforce your dog's response *after* it has left the bowl alone.

6   Repeat steps 2 to 5 a few times with boring food in the dish, such as diced carrots, and then more appealing things such as dry food.

7   Progress to a point where you can place a bowl on the ground which contains the dog's usual meal. Say 'leave it' as usual.

Teaching your dog to wait for its meal

When your young child starts feeding the dog, use a light plastic dish and ask an older child or adult to supervise the activity each time.

8   Pause for a few seconds before saying 'yours', or whatever word you wish, as you point to the food bowl.

Practising the lesson

9   Gradually increase the time between putting the bowl down and saying 'yours'. Vary this length of time each day, so the dog cannot predict how long it will have to wait.

Possible problems	Possible causes	Suggested remedies
The dog grabs food from the dish before you have said 'yours'.	You are progressing too quickly from an empty dish to the dog's meal.	Go back to using an empty bowl. Offer the dog a morsel of its favourite food from your hand as you put the dish down. Then progress from there to boring food, then to the dog's usual meal.

References

American Veterinary Medical Association (AVMA), 'Task force on canine aggression and human-canine interactions: A community approach to dog bite', *Veterinary Medicine Today*, vol. 218(11), 2001, pp. 1733–1749.

Bandura, A. *Principles of Behaviour Modification*, Holt, Rinehart & Winston, New York, 1969.

Bandura, A. *Social Foundations of Thought and Action: A Social Cognitive Theory*, Prentice Hall, Englewood Cliffs, New Jersey, 1986.

Barrett, J. *The Human/Companion Animal Bond*. Web page: <www.isis.csuhayward.edu/ALSS/soc/NAN/dd/6800jb/jbanbond.htm>

Coleman, G.J., Hall, M.J. & Hay, M. 'An evaluation of the responsible pet ownership program for schools' (Pre-publication copy).

Davey, G. *Animal Learning and Conditioning*, The Macmillan Press, London, 1981.

Gerald, K. & Gerald, D. *Counselling Children: A Practical Introduction*, Sage Publications, London, 1998.

Gething, L., Papalia, D.E. & Olds, S.W. *Life Span Development*, McGraw-Hill Book Company, Sydney, 1995.

Harris, M.J. & Rosenthal, R. 'Mediation of interpersonal expectancy effects: 31 meta analyses', *Psychological Bulletin*, vol. 97, 1985, pp. 363–386.

Katcher, A. 'Physiologic and behavioral responses to companion animals', *Veterinary Clinics of North America: Small Animal Practice*, vol. 15 (2), 1985, pp. 403–410.

Lepper, M.R. & Greene, D. *The Hidden Costs of Reward: New Perspectives on the Psychology of Human Motivation*, Wiley, New York, 1978.

Miller, R.L., Brickman, P. & Bolen, D. 'Attribution versus persuasion as a means for modifying behaviour', *Journal of Personality and Social Psychology*, vol. 31, 1975, pp. 430–441.

O'Farrell, V. *Manual of Canine Behaviour*, British Small Animal Veterinary Association, Gloucestershire, 1992.

Ozanne-Smith, J., Ashby, K. & Stathakis, V. 'Dog bites and injury prevention: A critical review and research agenda'. Animals, Community Health and Public Policy Symposium, University of Sydney, 27 November 1998.

Pavlov, I. *Conditioned Reflexes*, Dover, New York, 1960.

Piaget, J. *The Origins of Intelligence in the Child*, Norton, New York, 1963.

Rogers, C. *Freedom to Learn*, Merrill, Columbus Ohio, 1969.

Rosenthal, R. & Jacobson, L. *Pygmalion in the Classroom*, Holt, Rinehart & Winston, New York, 1968.

Scott, J. & Fuller, J. *Dog Behavior: The Genetic Basis*, The University of Chicago Press, Chicago, 1965.

Serpell, J. *In the Company of Animals: A Study of Human–Animal Relationships*, Cambridge University Press (Canto), Cambridge, 1996 (2nd edition).

Skinner, B.F. *About Behaviorism*, Vintage Books, New York, 1978.

Vaughan, D. 'Canine color vision', *American Kennel Gazette*, May 1991, pp. 52–58.

Weston, D. *Dog Training: The Gentle Modern Method*, Hyland House, Melbourne, 1990.

Weston, D. & Weston, R. *Dog Problems: The Gentle Modern Cure*, Hyland House, Melbourne, 1992.

Weston, D. & Weston, R. *Your Ideal Dog: Teach Your Best Friend to be a Perfect Companion*, Hyland House, Melbourne, 1997.

Acknowledgements

First and foremost, we would like to thank all of the members of The Kintala Club and The Australian Association of Gentle Modern Dog Training Instructors (AAGMDTI) for being such great ambassadors for The Gentle Modern Method of Dog Training™. Some of you, most notably Diane Godfrey and Alison Tuxworth, have been spreading the word for more than twenty-five years now; an amazing effort especially given all the other commitments in your busy lives.

In the early days many Kintala Club members were denigrated for daring to be different and moving away from the compulsive method of training using choker chains. These days training using positive reinforcement is almost accepted as the norm – but we still need to stand true to our philosophies and continue to share our learnings with others. Without the hard work and dedication of all Kintala members, but particularly the past and present instructors and committee members, thousands of people and dogs would not have had the benefit of such a rewarding friendship.

The photographs in the book add great appeal and we would like to thank the late David Weston for his dedication, not only to dogs and dog training, but also for putting so much effort into getting the best images possible. We extend our deepest gratitude for all of his work.

We needed many new photographs of kids and dogs for this book and were extremely fortunate to find a friend and professional photographer who could help us. At the time Wendy Mitchell was starting up her own business but had already gained considerable experience photographing dog events. Wendy certainly disproved the adage 'don't work with children and dogs' as she calmly worked her way through the schedule of shots we had organised. Thank you Wendy.

The kids who acted as our major 'models' for the photos really were fantastic – thank you to Kimberley, Boris, Freya, Robbie, Dhillon and Chandler, children of Kintala Club members. The adult club members who took part recently and in the past are too numerous to mention but we are eternally grateful for their time and cooperation. We hope you enjoy the results.

Special thanks to veterinarians/club members Drs Tim Adams and Karen Budd, who provided us with the images of baby Ella and their Nova Scotia Duck Tolling Retrievers, Abby and Astro, which appear in Chapter 8 and elsewhere.

Our publishing team at Allen & Unwin were terrific and highly professional. We were kept constantly informed and involved as the book progressed through typesetting and design – to final result. We had the value of input from many talented people who shared their insights, and challenged us to see things differently. This book is so much better for their time and commitment. Thank you Sue, Clare, Rachel, Sandra and Andrea.

Before we began this book, we asked many Kintala Club members, family and friends to complete a questionnaire about what they would like to see in a book on kids and dogs. Many people candidly shared their thoughts with us and their ideas and experiences helped to shape this book. We extend our sincere thanks.

We would not have the knowledge about psychology, learning and dog behaviour if it were not for the ground-breaking efforts of researchers and scientists of the past. In particular we acknowledge the seminal works of B.F. Skinner, Ivan Pavlov, John Scott and John Fuller, Jean Piaget and Albert Bandura.

Ruth was also lucky enough to study wolves at Wolf Park, Battle Ground, USA. Some of her updated knowledge about wolves acquired during this visit is now incorporated in AAGMDTI instructor training courses. Thanks to Erich Klinghammer (Ethologist) and staff.

Finally – to the dogs that have taught us, and given us, so much over the years. Without you our lives would be so much poorer.

Ruth Weston and Catriona Ross PhD.
April 2004

How to contact us in Australia

The Gentle Modern School of Dog Training

- Individual private training for puppies and adult dogs
- Help with behaviour problems
- Friendly advice
- State Government-approved instructors

To find out more – please phone:
Ruth Weston **(03)9439 8546 AH**

The Kintala Club Inc. (founded 1976)

Promoting responsible dog ownership in a friendly, non-competitive way.
State Government-approved instructors.

What does the club offer?

- Puppy training course from 8 weeks of age
  You will learn to teach your dog to:
      come when called
      behave well with people and other dogs
      sit, stand and lie down on signal
      stay in the above positions
      fetch and give up a toy
- Ideal Dogs of Australia courses – a State Government-approved course developed to assist you to teach your dog to be a well-behaved and accepted member of the community
- Ongoing training and socialisation for dogs of all ages whether pure or cross bred
- 10 different levels of training from beginners to advanced
- Our famous Canine Commando course
- Pets as Therapy training
- Tracking and scent work
- Regular informative magazines
- Lots of friendship and fun for you and your dog, and much, much more

To find out more – please phone:
Ruth Weston **(03)9439 8546 AH**
Chris or Tina Foster **(03)9489 6814**
Helen Morris **(03)9890 8626**
Diane Godfrey **(03)9438 6004 AH**
Website **‹http://avoca.vicnet.net.au/~kintala/›**

Kids and K9s program

A Kintala-sponsored community program for kindergartens and primary schools mainly in northern metropolitan Melbourne. Kids are taught how to:

- read canine body language
- behave safely around dogs – this includes role play

Kids have the opportunity to meet and pat a friendly dog.

To find out more – please phone:
Daniela Sandmann **(03)9710 1817**

The Australian Association of Gentle Modern Dog Training Instructors Inc.

The Association is an umbrella organisation responsible for providing:

- approved dog training courses under State Government legislation
- instructor-training courses. Instructors who successfully complete the course are accredited under the Domestic (Feral and Nuisance) Animals Act.

To find out more – please phone:
Barbara Swarbrick **(03)9480 3735**
Alan Smith **(03)9438 4343**

Professional photography

To find our more – please phone:
Wendy Mitchell **(03)5261 3391, 0409 440 668**
P.O. Box 46 Torquay 3228

**Previous best-selling books by David and Ruth Weston,
featuring the internationally recognised
Gentle Modern Method of Training™.**

Dog Training: The Gentle Modern Method
(Hyland House, Melbourne, 1990)
Over 100,000 copies sold
Train your dog quickly and easily. Over twenty lessons are featured,
from the basics to the advanced exercises required for obedience trials.
Suitable for puppies as young as eight weeks of age as well as adult dogs.
More than eighty photos illustrate the step-by-step instructions
so the book can be used successfully by both beginners and
advanced dog trainers.

Dog Problems: The Gentle Modern Cure
(Hyland House, Melbourne, 1992)
Over 70,000 copies sold
Do you have a dog that won't come when it is called, chases cats, joggers
or bikes, chews furniture, pulls madly on the lead or has any of the many
problems which dogs develop in our society? If so – this is the book for
you! More than 120 colour photos illustrate how you can influence your
dog to *want* to change its bad habits!

*Your Ideal Dog:
Teach Your Best Friend to be a Perfect Companion*
(Hyland House, Melbourne, 1997)
Do you want a dog that always comes when it is called,
walks politely on the lead, doesn't run off when you tell it to stay and is
sociable towards other dogs and people of all ages? In ten easy lessons,
you will learn how to educate your dog for life in the twenty-first century.
You will also be able to undertake the various assessments
throughout Australasia, the USA and UK.